D1718961

WE'RE SMART. WE'RE OLD.
AND WE'RE
THE BEST AT EVERYTHING.

The World's First No–BS Guide to
Legal Marketing and Branding

BY ROSS FISHMAN, JD

We're Smart. We're Old. And We're The Best At Everything.
The World's First No-BS Guide to Legal Marketing and Branding

Published by Fishman Marketing, Inc.

ISBN 978-0-9979676-3-0

Cover Design by Tony Bonilla and Michelle Benjamin
Book Design by Michelle Benjamin

DEDICATION

This book is dedicated to my extraordinary wife, **Kitty.** Twenty-seven years ago, she was nine-months pregnant with our first child. The very day we moved into our first home, I told her that I wanted to quit my lucrative litigation career for an entry-level marketing job that wouldn't even cover our bills—and she told me to follow my passion. And to our four amazing kids, **Andrew, Rob, Jonathan,** and **Elyssa,** who literally grew up in law firm marketing. They've traveled the world with me, attending conferences and listening to my speeches and showing me that they're each unique and special and wonderful.

And to **Dan, Eric,** and **Tony**—Fishman Marketing's evil geniuses—whose brilliant creative ideas grace these pages. They have ensured that our clients' work stands far above their competition and changed the face of global law firm marketing.

Finally, a special shout-out to Fishman Marketing's Creative Director, the amazing **Michelle Benjamin,** whose design expertise, preternatural work ethic, and unquestioning loyalty makes it a delight and honor to have her in our lives.

PRAISE FOR
"WE'RE SMART. WE'RE OLD. AND WE'RE THE BEST AT EVERYTHING."

For law firms to *be* like businesses, they must learn to *market*
like businesses. Law firms can find their courage and roadmap
inside these pages. *Fishman has finally written down
what has been inside his wonderfully creative mind these last 25 years*
and is sharing it with the rest of us. Don't miss it!
Bryan Schwartz, Chairman and Co-Founder, **Levenfeld Pearlstein**

Ross is a true innovator.
His iconoclastic views on lawyers and marketing are enlightening
and *his book provides a no-nonsense, common sense, and entertaining
guide to success* from an elite marketer who has mastered his craft.
Dean N. Gerber, Vice Chair, **Vedder Price**

*Ross' masterful book gives lawyers successful formulas and practical insights
to differentiate themselves and grow their businesses.*
His humorous style and straightforward approach will have
you eager to implement his ideas without delay.
Maggie Watkins, CMO, **Sedgwick, LLP**
1999 LMA President

A must-read for any attorney who wants to develop business.
This entertaining quick read demonstrates the concepts
that Ross has successfully implemented for law firms
around the world. Ross' methods are effective whether you
are a newbie attorney or a seasoned veteran.
Wonderful examples, case studies, and pictures allow Ross
to convey his ideas in a simple and easy-to-understand manner.
Jordan M. Goodman, Marketing Partner, **Horwood Marcus & Berk**

Ross tells it like it is. From the beginning you are drawn in and find
yourself commenting out loud, mostly in agreement. His examples
are real life, which both attorneys and marketers can relate to.
This is a must-read book.
Marcie Johnson, former Marketing Director, **Chapman & Cutler,**
1991 President NALFMA/LMA

Ross was the first consultant I worked with when I started in legal marketing almost 20 years ago. *His no-nonsense approach was a breath of fresh air then and remains so today.* The world of legal services has changed significantly and continues to evolve. Ross' message was spot on then and still is now. Differentiation is king and innovation is its queen.
Aleisha Gravit, CMO, **Akin Gump Strauss Hauer & Feld, 2013 LMA President**

Ross delivers again! To say that Ross has been and there and done that in the world of legal marketing would be a gross understatement. *Decades of wisdom are delivered in a funny, insightful, and practical way that makes this essential reading for the legal marketing industry.*
Nat Slavin, co-founder **Wicker Park Group, 2007 LMA President**

Read Ross' book! I am a (grateful) client of Ross Fishman and his marketing team. His creative, smart work helped me build my law practice into something I always hoped for, but didn't know how to achieve.
Brian J. Lewis, founding partner, **Gibson & Lewis**

"As with the Constitution, Ross Fishman's marketing strategies are living, breathing rules of success not otherwise constricted by traditional concepts. His recognition of the law's changing landscape has resulted in *a comprehensive handbook of timely and tactical applications to legal marketing ideas.*"
G. Steven Henry, Founder and General Counsel, **Litigation Counsel of America (LCA)**

There are an abundance of legal marketing publications these days. Sadly, I am forced to report that they are tedious, lackluster affairs which function best as soporifics. Ross Fishman's new book is *cheeky, deeply intelligent, and chock-a-block full of clear thinking about marketing your law firm,* underpinned by fun and true examples of accomplishing these objectives. *It is a living, breathing guide to smart marketing.* And it mirrors Ross Fishman's own ability to partner with firms while keeping a smile in words and deeds. So throw away all the marketing detritus filling your shelves and inboxes and settle in for some authentic assistance. *Much like Ross, this book rocks!*
Diane Hamlin, Former CMO, **Fenwick & West, 2005 LMA President**

ABOUT THE AUTHOR

"MANY PEOPLE CONSIDER ROSS FISHMAN TO BE THE NATION'S FOREMOST EXPERT ON LAW FIRM MARKETING."

–Of Counsel

Ross Fishman, JD is CEO of Fishman Marketing, specializing in strategy, branding, websites, and marketing training for law and professional-services firms. A former litigator, marketing director, and marketing partner, he has helped 200 law firms dominate their markets worldwide. A Fellow of the College of Law Practice Management, Ross was the first marketer to receive the Legal Marketing Association's "Lifetime Achievement" award, and the first inductee into the LMA's international "Hall of Fame."

A five-time winner of the Legal Marketing Association's "Best in Show" grand prize and Kentucky Colonel, he is a highly rated keynote speaker and marketing trainer, having spoken 300 times on six continents and written 250 bylined articles on legal marketing and branding issues. His popular book "The Ultimate Law Firm Associate's Marketing Checklist," is available on Amazon.com at goo.gl/HsrmbE (Chapter One is included at the end of this book).

CONTACT ROSS at ross@fishmanmarketing.com or +1.847.432.3546.

SUBSCRIBE to Ross' blog at fishmanmarketing.com/blog.

SOCIAL MEDIA:
> **Linkedin**.com/in/rossfishman
> **Twitter** at @rossfishman
> **Facebook**.com/fishmanmarketing

IN MEMORIUM

MARC A. YUSSMAN (1958-2008)
GOLDBERG SIMPSON, LOUISVILLE, KY

The best marketing partner ever

*To the administrator who denied our
request for a $250 color printer many years ago
because "Lawyers don't need color."*

FOREWORD

So it's early 1990 and a young blond man wearing a neat pinstriped suit walks into my office. I was the newly minted marketing partner at Winston & Strawn. It was a typically cold, damp, dank, and windy winter day in Chicago.

My visitor was Ross Fishman, and my long and largely unproductive day quickly took a turn for the better. The fellow had that spark of personality, ready smile, and gift of gab that define a live wire. I sensed this right from the start.

Ross proved to be an invaluable colleague. It seems that he'd recognized before most of us that common corporate practices like branding, differentiation, and standing apart from the crowd in a commoditized industry apply to the practice of law. He found his life's work: teaching lawyers and law marketers at all levels of experience how to develop and expand business.

Now Ross' wise counsel is in book form and the book is in your hands. Do not put it down! For despite his legal training, his law degree, and bar membership, his writing is clear, concise, free of clichés, and as easy to digest as a chewable vitamin. Anecdotes, examples (both positive and negative), humor, and pathos leap off the pages of this volume. They will help you find clients and their hearts, minds, and wallets. This book is a bargain at twice the price.

I read this book. I laughed. I cried. I lost 10 pounds.

Try it—you'll like it!

Loren A. Wittner
Former Marketing Partner, Winston & Strawn

Phoenix, Arizona
February 2017

PREFACE

Does it drive you crazy that big-firm lawyers can charge 30-50 percent more per hour than you? *You* know you're just as skilled, but the marketplace doesn't, so you charge $100 or $250 less for every single hour. Hour after hour. Day after day. Month after month.

Calculate how much more revenue that totals every single year. Go ahead, I'll wait….

Is that *frustrating?*

Actually, that's *branding.*

And *that's* what this book is about.

I want you to aspire to *more*. To *look* different. To *be* different. I want you or your firm to create a brand that helps you get more out of your career.

I want you to represent better clients, charge more money, and have more fun. To build a rewarding, fulfilling career as a market leader. I want you to figure out how to offer something more, and then tell that story persuasively to your potential buyers. This book will show you how.

Good luck, I hope you enjoy it. Please feel free to contact me any time if you have questions at ross@fishmanmarketing.com.

Ross

Ross Fishman

Highland Park, IL
February 2017

INTRODUCTION _____

Marketing isn't easy, and branding is harder still. But its inherent difficulty is what makes it so powerful; it ensures that only the savviest firms can wield this strategic weapon.

When training lawyers in marketing, I've found that they learn best when I:

(1) Provide a new idea they might not have previously considered,
(2) Explain the underlying theory, then
(3) Show a bunch of actual examples.

So that's how we structured this book, in two sections:

PART ONE starts by explaining the basic concepts of marketing, branding, and differentiation; identifies a variety of common issues or challenges; provides some background; and uses real-life examples from leading law firms to show how we solved those problems.

PART TWO details dozens of common marketing and branding challenges and how we addressed them for specific firms, hopefully providing some guidance for firms that find themselves facing a similar situation.

And we always show lots of cool pictures.

TABLE OF CONTENTS

PART ONE: BRANDING AND DIFFERENTIATION

TABLE OF CONTENTS

PART TWO: CASE STUDIES

Excerpt of

"THE ULTIMATE LAW FIRM ASSOCIATE'S MARKETING CHECKLIST"

PART ONE

BRANDING & DIFFERENTIATION

CHAPTER ONE

INTRODUCTION:
UNDERSTANDING THE MARKETING UMBRELLA

MAY WE NEVER HEAR ANOTHER LAWYER SPOUT: "MY FIRM HAS A COLLEGIATE CULTURE."

Not that long ago, lawyers thought marketing was distasteful and unprofessional. The best lawyers didn't need to look for work—their reputations would precede them, and word-of-mouth referrals would simply come. "Doing good work is the best marketing." And for generations of lawyers, that was generally true.

When demand dramatically outstrips supply, every year is a good year. It can be easy to think you're doing everything right. And some firms were. But most firms, without realizing it, were simply riding the wave that propelled every firm forward.

Why radically change your marketing when last year was "Our most-profitable year ever!" and you raised your rates *another* ten percent? It's hard to argue with that logic.

As we know, the good old days are long gone. The tides turned; supply now exceeds demand. Competition is fierce from all sides—not just from the look-alike firms down the street, but from inventive or alternative providers like Axiom, Rocket Lawyer, Docracy, and LegalZoom. Technology solutions and off-shore firms are chewing up the low-end bread-and-butter work, while IBM's Watson and AI companies simultaneously attack the high end. Carpet-bagging regional firms move into new geographic markets. New law school grads are entering a glutted market, the unlucky bastards.

Today, quality work by experienced lawyers is the price of admission. It's a given. The world is full of capable lawyers, and being talented barely gets you in the game. The firms that couldn't skillfully depose a witness, broker a deal, or draft a workable contract are long gone. These days you have to do more than perform your job well. You must step up, stand out, and *win* the business.

Studies show that after clients create their short lists, they decide which lawyer to select from that list, and "reputation" is one of the top few criteria, in addition to "expertise" and "chemistry." Marketing consultants, like my associates and me and our friends at other consultancies can't improve your courtroom or bargaining-table skills. We certainly can't improve your personality. But through our marketing efforts we can help you create and showcase your reputation. *This* we can do.

Do you want more out of your career? Do you want to stand out from the crowd? Are you ready to become a *leader* and make more money? Do you want to spend the rest of your career doing work you love, for clients you enjoy? Or work you enjoy for clients you love? If you do, this book will show you *precisely* how to accomplish this, in relatively short order.

And, surprisingly, it can actually be *fun*. Many older-generation partners don't see the fun in marketing—although I've met plenty who do—but younger, enlightened lawyers have caught on. There's no reason why most attorneys and their marketers can't become proficient at building a proud, prominent reputation.

Around 1992, I was a marketing professional inside Winston & Strawn, a large, Chicago-based law firm. We ran a pretty dull advertisement that ran in the very first issue of the publication *Corporate Legal Times* (now *Inside Counsel*). A generic, four-word headline ("Committed to Client Service"), eight words of self-evident text ("A national law firm for the business community"), and a list of our cities and phone numbers. LOTS of empty white space.

WE'RE SMART. WE'RE OLD. AND WE'RE THE BEST AT EVERYTHING.

The firm's Marketing Committee was outraged. They considered all that white space a waste of money. Worse, the font was a *sans serif* (that is, it didn't have those little "feet"). Law firms couldn't use a sans serif font! Law firms must use Courier, so the materials looked like they were clacked out on an Olivetti typewriter! (No really, we had this actual argument.)

Eventually, we won the debate and some national marketing awards. Because at that time, all the other firms *were* using Courier—even the simple Times New Roman font was considered scandalous. And the other firms filled their ads margin-to-margin with single-spaced, self-aggrandizing puffery, theoretically squeezing every dollar of value out of the advertisement. In the magazine, our light, airy ad stood out like a stop sign in a dictionary.

And that's the whole point: You shouldn't be like everyone else. You should seek to rise above the competition.

Today, 25+ years later, law firm marketing has exploded in variety and quality. We've gone from a staid black-and-white world to a world of color and creativity. International firm logos use unexpected and previously spurned colors like orange, yellow, pink, and purple. The sky's now the limit on innovation and differentiation—and your top challengers are using them to target your best clients.

Good marketing should help you or your firm rise above the competition. It should show how you're different from other firms, and how you're better for a particular type of case, matter, industry, or client. It should help you dominate your chosen market. Not simply "attract more business." *Dominate.*

Marketing starts with a message tailored to fit your particular brand. The brand is what you want people to know about you—that crucial, defining factor that sets you apart or makes you worthy of their attention and money. You devise a strategy for disseminating that message, choosing among a range of media to teach your audience that crucial thing about you and your firm.

The complete range of tools is now readily available to do this. Leading firms—once afraid to use color in their marketing—are using them ingeniously and aggressively to significantly increase awareness, revenue, and profits. Still think corporate-style marketing is "unprofessional"? Prominent lawyers and firms have used attention-getting marketing devices as varied as these:

- Lawyer baseball cards and autographed baseballs
- Private-label video games
- Logo'd insects, condoms, and bib overalls
- "Misplaced" wallets with business cards inside
- Direct-mail hot peppers
- Bathroom-mirror stickers
- Photo postage stamps
- Logo'd test tubes and martini shakers
- Sponsoring PGA golfers, NASCAR drivers, and cricket players
- Billboards showing lingerie models
- Seed-packet business cards
- Logo'd defused hand grenades (oops)
- Product placement on television dramas
- Moving billboards
- Comic book-styled new-business proposals
- An employment law blog that deconstructed each episode of "The Office"
- A specialty in defending corporations from tweets by President Trump
- Practice-specific microsites (see pages 6-7)

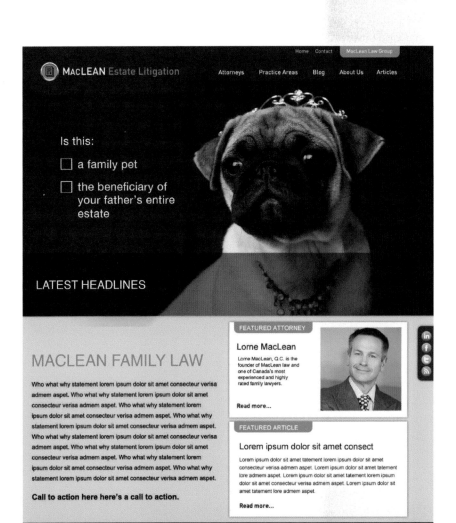

Having problems with your will? MacLEAN Estate Litigation
www.bcfamilylaw.ca

It's not about money.
It's about justice.

Then money.

From medical malpractice to serious personal injury and wrongful death, you never think that it will happen to you. When it does, talk to us and we'll fight to get you the personal injury settlement you need to heal.

MacLEAN Personal Injury
www.bcfamilylaw.ca

See more on pages 93-95

A new marketing campaign starts with explicit knowledge of what your firm is about, what it does best, and what it wants and needs to say. Recently, for example, we rolled out a new marketing and branding campaign for Chicago's leading estate-planning law firm, a 30-lawyer boutique called Hoogendoorn and Talbot. While "estate planning" is the substantive category they fit into, there's so much more to the firm. It's my job as a branding consultant to figure out who they are, what they do, and how they do it, then tell that story in a way that a particular target audience finds enticing.

Gathering that information is the first step in telling a lawyer or firm's story so it resonates. Any good branding consultant should do this. To create as detailed a picture as possible, we start by conducting meticulous one-on-one interviews to learn about the firm, its lawyers, and their individual practices. It all stems from the questions. *Who is this firm? Who are their clients? What are they trying to accomplish? Where are they going to generate revenue? What are they looking to become? What do they want from their practice?*

We spend a lot of time gaining a nuanced understanding of the firm's culture, style, and personality. If you don't hire us or another branding professional to help you carry out an extensive analysis of your firm and its operations and culture, you should do it yourself, as formally and candidly as you can. You need to know who you are and what you stand for. And critical self-examination is always a challenge.

In gathering information and getting to know Hoogendoorn and Talbot, for example, we discovered that it's a devoutly religious firm, with a Lutheran, faith-based environment. This mindset is important to them, and we needed to understand their core beliefs and values.

We also familiarized ourselves with the culture and personalities of their target audiences. For Hoogendoorn and Talbot, those audiences can be referral sources like other lawyers and law firms, accounting firms, and financial planners, as well as the affluent entrepreneurs, elderly widows, and other clients the firm helps directly with estate-planning issues.

A firm designing a marketing strategy needs to undergo a lot of analysis and introspection to understand what it is that the firm stands for. Lawyers should ask themselves: *What is special about me? About us? Why are we here at this particular firm? What is it about these lawyers that I have affinity with? What are our primary values?* The answers must be something other than sappy clichés about "providing quality service" or "good lawyers doing good work to keep clients happy." And, please, no one is allowed to describe their culture as "collegial." If I hear a lawyer utter the phrase "our collegial [or worse, 'collegiate'] culture" one more time, I'm going to…arrrrrrgggggh!

Okay, let me take a deep breath and simply say that many, perhaps most, lawyers spew bland pablum in characterizing their firms and practices. Instead, you must know what sets you and/or your firm apart from every other lawyer or firm. (I'll cover this more in a subsequent chapter.)

PULLING IT ALL TOGETHER, CONNECTING EVERYONE INVOLVED

From the information that emerges from our inquiries, we stitch together a brand message that resonates with every member of the firm, regardless of their practice or personality. We have to understand who each person is so we can find the thread that connects them all together. When we launch their marketing campaign we want these attorneys to exclaim: "Yes, that sounds like me and my practice!" We want them to be proud of the message and logo and feel connected to both. We want them to be excited to hand out their business cards because they're proud of what the design says about them as a lawyer.

In the case of an estate-planning firm such as Hoogendoorn and Talbot, lawyers and their clients are dealing with very personal and sensitive subjects, including family relationships, finances, inheritances, multi-generational dynamics—and sometimes conflicts. In a wealthy family, for example, the first generation of hard-charging, driven entrepreneurs who started the business is very different than the third generation, which has grown up accustomed to the high standard of living provided by the family business that is getting passed down to subsequent generations. We must consider these types of details when we develop a firm's brand and its message.

The information-gathering process produces a clear image of the firm's character, which helps us craft a new logo. In the case of Hoogendoorn and Talbot, the distinctive shape and spelling of first name of the firm—Hoogendoorn—lent itself to an interesting design.

In getting to know the firm we realized that the firms' attorneys often stepped into roles beyond just "lawyer." They worked the intersection of two different areas. Each was a lawyer *plus*—a lawyer and a therapist, a lawyer and a referee, a lawyer and a financial advisor. Playing off this duality, we designed a logo that turns the double o's in "Hoogendoorn" into a representations of Venn diagrams, to symbolize that the lawyers' practice falls at the intersection of different areas of expertise.

HⵔOGENDⵔORN
& TALBOT LLP

Although the Hoogendoorn logo plays off an abstract-logic concept, we also wanted to convey that the firm is warm, welcoming, and caring—exactly what people want from estate-planning experts. In addition, the firm sincerely focuses on diversity. All these pieces come together in the marketing campaign, which combines the brand platform Venn-diagram strategy with beautiful photos of multi-ethnic, multi-generational families.

BEFORE

AFTER

Hoogendoorn & Talbot lawyers know that to be successful when representing families and individuals, you must be more than just one thing. As Chicago's leading estate-planning law firm, we are right there at the center, protecting our clients from whatever comes at them, with experience, faith, and the confidence that comes from both. **Please call us at 312.786.2250 or visit us at hoogendoom.com**

HOOGENDOORN
& TALBOT LLP

INTERSECT WITH US

We took that strategic foundation and transformed it into other marketing tools, including a tag line: *Planning the Future.* That's integral to who the firm is, how they feel about themselves and their work, and how they tell their story.

The visuals are also turned into other outreach tools, such as direct mailers, websites, and LinkedIn profiles and other social media outlets. For Hoogendoorn and Talbot, the images illustrated the print ads the firm uses to advertise to Chicago-area lawyers for referrals and lateral hiring.

Finally, I want to say that this entire process is an exercise in aspiration. This endeavor should help you take the next step up, to not just say who you are, but who you'd like to become. If you're stuck acting in a certain way, it becomes who you are. When you strive for something beyond the status quo, you change. For the better.

CHAPTER TWO

ONLINE PRESENCE:
MAKING MARKETING MAGIC WITH WEBSITES

ADMIT IT, THE HOME PAGE CONVINCED YOU
THAT THE FIRM WAS SIMPLY AWFUL.

I stand in front of a wooden podium in a packed hotel conference room. The name-tagged lawyers and marketers take their seats and size me up.

The anxious conference organizer just informed me that some of the lawyer attendees are extremely skeptical of marketing. I assure her that that's always the case, not to worry. She says that a few especially vocal lawyers mercilessly heckled the previous speaker. I reassure her that it'll be fine.

So confident am I that the audience soon will be laughing out loud, having completely changed their fiercely held anti-marketing opinions in less than ten minutes, that I make a wager with her. I back up my claims with solid US currency: a nickel.

Granted, lawyers are a tough audience. They're smart, cynical, and quick studies. Although comfortable learning by sitting in a classroom, they bore easily and don't suffer fools. The material must be new, fresh, smart, practical, and fast paced.

Most lawyers today have accepted that some sort of marketing is necessary, if not important. There remain, of course, skeptics and gadflies, whose primary objection is that business clients, particularly executives and in-house lawyers, are too smart and cynical to fall for a law firm's marketing efforts.

Knowing this, I forge ahead:

"I'd like to start by getting us on the same page, to show what good marketing can, and should, accomplish for you or your firm. Let's say you meet an attorney at a professional conference or a seminar. You're impressed with her; she seems smart and skilled, and there's good chemistry. So, you do what most people would do—you ask for her business card. Later, back at work, you go to the lawyer's website to learn a little more about her and her firm.

"You type in the URL, and see *this*:

"As you click through the different pages of the website, you're subconsciously asking yourself some questions:

- *"What do I think of this firm?*
- *"What kind of firm are they?*
- *"What's my overall impression?*
- *"What kind of building are they in?*
- *"What does their lobby look like?*
- *"What kind of furniture do they have?*
  "Is it elegant? Modern? Formal? Expensive?
  Old and tired? Ratty?
- *"Where did my acquaintance go to law school?*
- *"What do I think about the nature of her practice?*
- *"What kind of cases does she handle?*
- *"How does she handle them?*
- *"If I had a bet-the-company piece of litigation,*
  is this a firm I would trust to handle that?
- *"If I had a precedent-setting issue that I couldn't afford to lose,*
  is this the kind of firm I would hire?

"Now, this is an experienced firm," I say, "and it provides quality client service—it says so right there on the website."

I show the parts of the site where the firm brags about itself, the parts that say things like: "We're experienced," "We're client-oriented," "We're your partners," or some variation on those themes.

"They say that they're 'experienced'… but do you believe them? It's on the Internet, so it must be true, right?"

A few audience members chuckle.

"Now if you had to rate this firm on a one-to-ten scale for quality of the lawyers' technical skills, with one being 'terrible' and ten being 'terrific,' what number would you give them? Think about it. Really, give them a number."

I pause.

"A show of hands, please—who would give them a 6-to-10 score? … Nobody? All right, nobody gives them a 6-to-10."

"Okay," I ask, "Who would give them a 1 to 5? … Almost everybody."

Now I get more specific.

"Who would give them a 1? How about a 2? A few twos. Who'd give them a 3? Ooh, lots of threes.

"A 4? Okay, some fours. 5? … Almost all 3s, and a few 4s. Around a 3.5 overall."

I pause again.

"So a 3.5 out of 10, so they're somewhere around a C-minus, perhaps a D-plus in terms of skill."

It's time for more slides. "Now take a look at this firm," I say.

I click through parts of this website.

"Same questions…You meet someone at a party or a conference. You think they're smart. You go to their website. What do you think of this firm? What about the quality of their skills? What is the nature of their practice? If you had a bet-the-company piece of litigation, would you hire them?"

"Here are some of the smiling biography photos, they seem like nice people:"

We go through the same basic questions.

"So what do you think of them? Who would give them a 1 to 5?" … No hands rise.

"How about a 6? No? How about a 7? OK, a lot of 7s. An 8? Some 8s. How about a 9? A few 9s. A 10? No, of course not, no lawyers ever give anybody a 10," I say. Laughter.

The ranking of 7.5 seems to be the audience consensus. Around a B+/A-. And then I do The Big Reveal. I show the home page of both sites together, side by side, the hackneyed, stale blue-and-white site juxtaposed alongside the strong "We Don't Blink" site.

The box that had hidden the firm name disappears to reveal that *it's the same firm.* … I've just showed them what a marketing makeover can do.

BEFORE

AFTER

The marketers in the audience smile. Many of the lawyers tilt their heads, looking confused.

The lawyers had just confidently rated the quality of what they thought were two different firms, resulting in one C- and one A-, meaning they wouldn't have hired the "first" firm, but certainly might have hired the "second" firm.

A wave of realization washes over the audience.

The revelation that the two websites are from the same firm forces

them to concede that marketing does, in fact, work. I've just refuted the typical lawyer-driven cliché that "you can't market a law firm" because, as it turns out, you *can*—even to sophisticated legal types who are supposedly too smart to fall for that stuff.

Remember, they weren't asked to assess the quality of the firms' marketing or website; they were asked to calculate the quality of the lawyers' *technical skills*. They viewed one firm as being far superior to the other. And they felt quite confident inferring this simply from the design of the home page. That's pretty powerful.

Then comes the disclaimer. I admit my audience that a great website is not going to win you big clients and big cases. "Clients won't say: 'Hey, I love your website! So, would you handle my antitrust case?'"

But, if you have a sub-par "before" website, it can prevent your firm from getting its foot in the door. Candid clients readily admit, "Look, I can't hire you. I simply can't show your crappy website to my Board, because it makes you look like, well, a crappy firm. If the case goes south for any reason and the CEO looks at your website, it will reflect poorly on me and my decision making. I like you, but I'm not willing to take that risk." I've heard that exact conversation many times, almost verbatim.

That is, a crummy website can directly cost you high-value business. However ridiculous that feels, that's just today's reality. We are all busy; we're forced to make snap judgments, particularly with the vast amount of material we encounter online. That's the whole point of Malcolm Gladwell's best-selling book, "*Blink.*"

On the other hand, a high-quality website positions you as a high-quality firm. At least you've got a shot—you're in the running. Your site sets you apart from all those other firms with their tedious shots of gavels, globes, and skylines (more about those in the next chapter). Those firms all look alike, and yours doesn't. Your firm stands for something. Something positive. Something *different*.

This particular website makeover I featured at the conference was a project we did for Hedrick Gardner, a Charlotte, NC-based firm that was seeking to add more high-dollar business litigation. The purpose of the website makeover wasn't to generate business, although it did do that, as a pleasant side effect. It was to recruit business litigators, to get lateral hires to sign with the firm.

Hedrick Gardner had been doing about 60 percent workers' compensation and 40 percent insurance defense litigation. They were an outstanding firm with skilled trial attorneys. Lawyers with a comp or insurance practice grow up regularly handling tough trials or administrative hearings. But insurance companies only paid maybe $150-$225 per hour for this work. Hedrick's trial lawyers were smart, efficient, hard working, and great at their jobs. And in court they regularly beat the crap out of big-name local and national firms who were billing their business clients at $650 an hour.

So, even though Hedrick Gardner lawyers were eminently qualified to handle sophisticated commercial litigation, they just couldn't get hired to do that work. The firm recognized the need to jump-start that practice by hiring top attorneys with established business-litigation practices. Unfortunately, firm management had been trying for many years to persuade these prospective laterals to join the firm, but they'd gotten no real interest.

Why was that? Their reputation was, accurately, as an insurance and comp firm. And that market is perceptually divided into two tiers: (1) the sophisticated high end that handles big, tough cases against great lawyers, and (2) the bottom-dwelling low end that handles low-dollar, high-volume cases.

The firm's website inadvertently positioned the firm in the latter category. Viewers could easily imagine the lawyers toiling unshaven, in ill-fitted brown suits and scuffed shoes, handling innumerable unsophisticated cases. And the best laterals at other firms aren't going to sign up for that.

Of course, that wasn't the reality of the sophisticated Hedrick Gardner practice. But if you say you're "terrific" but you look mediocre,

that's a dissonance that won't get resolved in your favor. People will believe what they see and feel, not what you say.

The remade website reflected Hedrick Gardner's dynamic culture, style, and personality. The lawyers there truly are nice people—but also tough, confident, strong, and highly experienced trial lawyers. My team and I were able to help them explain that they could handle business litigation similarly.

We didn't want the message to be: "We're not just insurance" because we didn't want to seem defensive about the nature of their history. We wanted to showcase what's great about an insurance-oriented practice—that it produces lawyers with significant, efficient trial skills. We turned those attributes and proficiencies into something marketable to business litigation and business litigators. In this situation, rather than talk about *what they do*, we focused on *how they do it*.

And it worked.

The website makeover was tremendously effective for lateral hiring. Within six months, Hedrick Gardner had hired a number of leading business litigators with books of business that gave them the traction they needed.

And that's the magic of marketing.

* * *

Back at the conference, my before-and-after exercise had taken maybe seven minutes. I could see the conference organizer standing in the back of the room. She was smiling at me, looking relieved.

Holding up a nickel.

CHAPTER THREE

BE TRUE TO WHO YOU ARE:
DON'T BLANKET YOUR MARKETING WITH CLICHÉS

IF I SEE A GAVEL OR STRIPED BOOK ON YOUR WEBSITE, I'M GOING TO SMACK YOU WITH IT.

While this book offers you many of the DOs in marketing, it also covers some of the equally important DON'Ts. I want to help you know what *not* to do when you market your firm. For example, *don't* rely on photos of smiling lawyers on your home page to differentiate your firm from your competitors. Photos of smiling lawyers will not convey your firm's message or culture or "commitment to clients." In fact, those images of friendly, neatly coiffed professional-looking men and women bearing their pearly whites will not convey *anything*.

Okay, that's not entirely true. The photos do say something. The message is: "Lawyers work here. Here's Joe, a litigator in our San Francisco office. [Fade out.] Here's Susan, a real estate lawyer in Chicago. Our firm has people. And they smile." And. That's. About. It.

You don't have to believe me. Go visit your top five competitors' websites (or maybe revisit your own site, as you might be guilty of this as well). It seems almost everybody is doing this. It's the latest law firm website cliché, and I want to discuss this further and show you how photography can enhance your web presence and set you apart.

But first I want to take a look at some marketing clichés of the past and share with you something I wrote decades ago in reference to law firm brochures (remember those?). It's still sadly relevant because most firms continue to use many of these hackneyed images. I refreshed the information in a two-part blog post titled "The Top 25 Law Firm Website Clichés to Avoid." online at *https://goo.gl/A0mnwr* and *https://goo.gl/lHYLWr*. In them, I point out that I think lawyers often are too literal for good marketing and tend to gravitate to the safe, obvious icons that represent the general concept of "Law," just like most of their closest competitors. I'll list the top ten here, and the trite messages I think that they convey. Ready?

1. A GLOBE OR A MAP

We're global!

Now, what the firm hopes to communicate here, of course, is that this partnership has international clients and practices globally. What might come to mind instead, however, is this: "We did a deal in Toronto once."

2. SHAKING HANDS

We're your partner!

The handshakes are firm, typically both male, and usually feature one light and one dark skin tone.

3. BUILDING/ARCHITECTURAL DETAIL

We work in a building!

I particularly enjoy this when it isn't even the firm's own building. No client ever said, "If I could just find a law firm that worked in a *building. That's* the firm I'd hire."

4. SKYLINES
We work in a city!

Oh, so *that's* how your firm is different than your competitors. *Your* firm works in a *city*. If you look carefully, you can often find another local firm using the exact same stock photo. I'd suggest that roughly 30 percent of law firms show one or more skylines. Sometimes more, representing their various offices. … Yawn.

5. COLUMNS/COURTHOUSE
We're lawyers!

This includes empty courtrooms and empty jury boxes. As my old friend and co-worker Russell Freund once said, "No one was ever confused by a photo of a column." Of course, no one was ever persuaded by it either.

6. GAVEL
Yup, we're lawyers.

I'm a lawyer. Here's my gavel.

7. LIGHTBULBS
We have good ideas!

This was arguably the very first lawyer visual cliché. Today they're spiral, energy-efficient LED bulbs. FYI, that's not better.

8. CHESS PIECES
We're strategic!

The king is often lying on his side. Sometimes they're attractively arranged on the board by a photographer who clearly never played chess. Here's a quick tip—bishops don't jump. This isn't checkers.

9. DIVERSE CONFERENCE ROOM
[INSERT Stock photo]

(Here's a stock photo of aggressively diverse, genetically perfect men and women of varying ethnicity who are obviously not lawyers, smiling.)

If you don't actually *have* any diversity, apparently some firms think it's enough to simply buy a $20 stock photo. You know, in solidarity.

10. VACANT LOBBY/CONFERENCE ROOM
It's 5:01.
We are OUT of here.
Or we have such high turnover that we can't take photos of our actual people.

Now it could be that your firm's guilty of running with one or more of these overused images. Well, the truth can be like a punch in the stomach sometimes. And, if that's the case, you may want to have a talk with your marketing committee.

GREAT IDEA OR A CONVENIENT ONE?
Speaking of marketing departments, here's how those smiling-lawyer photos find themselves wallpapering law firm websites. What happens in the marketing committee meetings is that someone makes this suggestion: "Hey, I've got a great idea. Let's use the lawyers in the photos." Usually that someone is the outside marketing consultant or web developer, who says, "Your people are so smart and handsome. Let's use them as the banner photos on the home page."

And then heads around the table start nodding vigorously in agreement—what a good idea! And everyone knows they won't get resistance from the attorneys. No lawyer ever blushed and said, "No, no, really. Please don't showcase me on the home page." Everyone in the room also understands how fortunate they'll be to decide on a visual in only one meeting. So it's an effortless and convenient choice, and it's easy to get the marketing committee to agree to that because, on the surface, it makes perfect sense. The expert loves it because it's his or her "great idea" and, more importantly, he or she can cash the check quickly and move on.

Rarely does someone stop the meeting and say, "Now wait a second. Aren't most of our competitors also doing that? How is that making us look different? How is that helping us? It's just burying us in the

mediocre middle."

Then when it comes time for the photo shoot, the photographer will choreograph the attorneys into a fake conference-room meeting scene. The photographer will direct the grouped attorneys: "All right everybody, on three, *look natural.* One, two, *three!*"

In truth, most people stiffen up when ordered to "look natural." Furthermore, many lawyers are not especially photogenic. No offense, but most of us didn't go to law school after rejecting a modeling offer by the Ford Agency. Photographers will tell them to "Pretend to have a conversation." And suddenly, the chattiest people in the world can't form a sentence. And in a photo of people talking, at least one or two will end up with their mouth open in an awkward, unattractive freeze frame. And what do I do with my hands? Maybe I'll just self-consciously gesticulate.

One of the newer photo clichés is the silhouette of someone in front of a window. That's a generic Business shot. It doesn't really say anything. All law firms have both people *and* windows. That doesn't tell me what you do or how you do it or how you do it better than the look-alike, sound-alike law firm across the street. But photographers like to shoot that one and lawyers like to use that one even though it's become one of those overused stock photos.

Or maybe you're familiar with this photo: A young, eager associate gazes adoringly at the wise older partner. I call this *The Mentoring Photo* and often I think it looks silly, at best, or downright creepy, at worst. It's even creepier when the senior male partner is looking down at a younger female associate who's seated at a desk. That's The Mentoring Photo that always looks like sexual harassment. It feels like he's preparing to offer her a shoulder massage.

When I give presentations to lawyers, law firm leaders and marketing directors, I'll talk about another photo you see way too often—a shot of a lawyer running up the courthouse steps. The law firm intends for the image to show that their attorneys are bold and aggressive and fast-paced and dynamic. But when I ask an audience, "What does this really say?" Many of the audience members will holler back, "Late for court!" Exactly. The potential client is probably thinking, "Hey Joe Attorney, next time wake up a few minutes earlier."

Another image that's become cliché appears on many firms' Energy practice web pages—the proverbial eco-friendly wind turbine or solar panel. A firm might have one lonely client who operates in the alternative-energy arena and 99 oil and gas companies, but that doesn't stop the partners from posting that photo of the green, easy-on-the-environment icon.

YOU CAN CHOOSE GENERIC AND "SAFE" OR DYNAMIC AND DARING

I'm often amazed at just how generic a firm's website is—and how badly it misses the mark in accurately reflecting the substance, style, personality, and presence of a particular firm. Consider the Howard Law Group, a small Michigan-based litigation boutique that tries big, difficult, complicated national cases and wins … and wins … and wins.

I met Bill Howard at a conference and was immediately impressed with his intelligence and persona. He's a big, tough, and frankly, scary-looking man. He's also a great guy, who's nice, smart, and funny. But he's got this bald bullet head and an intimidating presence. In talking to him, I learned that he has a trial record of roughly 300 wins to 4 losses, and that's only counting the major, complex cases, which include work for some of the nation's largest companies.

His website didn't convey that; it buried that important information, barely mentioning it. Frankly, the old website made Bill and his partners look like … pansies. It talked about the typical boring crap—client service, personal attention, approachability, the skills of a big firm in a smaller package, yadda yadda yadda. Here's the first thing a visitor would read when visiting that banal site:

"Experienced West Michigan trial lawyers. The Howard Law Group is a Grand Rapids, Michigan law firm that offers the talent, sophistication, and results you expect from a larger law firm with the high measure of accessibility and personal attention you expect from a smaller law firm."

That vanilla text missed the point and made it seem like they're provincial to the Grand Rapids area. They are anything but vanilla or small-town.

The photo of Bill on that site was lifeless. It was a forced awkward-smiling picture of him, and that's just not who he is. His partner Jean is also a "no BS" kind of person. Yet, in her photograph on the website, she looked light and frivolous.

Take a look and you'll see what I mean.

They look like nice, service-oriented lawyers—which they are—but nice, service-oriented lawyers are a dime a dozen. Bill consistently wins big, complex cases. *That* is the message. You don't want to hide that, rather, you want to lead with it. He's a bit of a bully in court. He takes on the other side and wears them down. He gets the points he wants to make, does so aggressively and forcefully—and juries love him. He also hates, that is, he HATES to lose.

Bill and Jean hired us to redesign their website. So we brought in a fashion photographer and retouched the photos to make them gritty. We were looking for grit with Bill because he is real. We weren't softening and putting Vaseline on the lens and touching up the photos to make him look pretty. He's wearing black, he's got a big watch, and he's looking straight down at you. He's got a don't-screw-with-me kind of expression. That's Bill. Now I want to be clear: He's a very charming guy with a great sense of humor, but he's also extremely competitive. Did I mention he hates to lose?

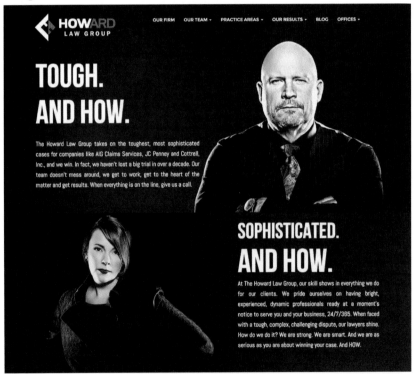

We wanted to show that when you need to win—when you simply can't afford to lose—you need to call this firm. So they need to look like tough winners. Why would you want to blather on about their client service, approachability, and accessibility? Screw that. And we leveraged the "How" in "Howard" in the headlines, "Tough. And How." "Sophisticated. And How."

Take a look for yourself.

We think the stark photography, unambiguous design, and active, no-nonsense text helps tell The Howard Law Group's story. And your website should tell *your* story. The redesigned site also differentiates the firm from its many competitors and their bland websites that spew passive and "safe" text, illustrated by gavels, columns, and skylines.

And all those smiling attorneys.

CHAPTER FOUR

EDUCATING THE LAWYERS:
FIRST TEACH WHAT MARKETING IS ALL ABOUT

LET'S GET REAL.
MOST LAWYERS' MARKETING INSTINCTS HERE ARE DEAD WRONG.

Lawyers are smart; they get it the first time. But when it comes to marketing, they just haven't had the class.

Let me say that again because it's critical to understand this if you want success as a marketer. In fact, it lies at the heart of the *single most-important thing I've learned in marketing.* I'll condense it this time: Lawyers are smart; they just haven't had the class.

Even these days, most attorneys don't understand marketing, let alone the important-yet-understated nuances that can make all the difference in grabbing the attention of potential clients and, ultimately, reeling them in.

Lawyers are not knowledgeable about marketing the way professional marketers are. We read articles and blog posts, we talk about it with friends and peers, we attend seminars and conferences. This is our industry so we eat, breathe, and think about this stuff 60 hours a week, year after year. Most lawyers pay attention to marketing, I don't know, maybe a couple hours per year? That's not really an exaggeration, at least for most attorneys. They just don't consider it an integral part of their job.

So it's up to us to educate our lawyers.

As I mentioned previously, in the early 1990s I worked in the marketing department of a terrific big firm, Winston & Strawn. I kept coming up with creative, effective ideas—something that, frankly, wasn't very difficult to do back then because law firm marketing was so new. Very few of the really good, innovative approaches had been used, so it was easy picking. But my ideas were consistently rejected. I kept thinking, "How can they be so *stupid?* How can they not see that this is obviously an effective, creative-but-not-too-far-out-there idea that would clearly generate significant revenue and interest in the firm? What is *wrong* with these people?" I was so frustrated.

Shortly after I received one of those rejections, we took a communications class at the firm. And that's when it hit me: I realized that most lawyers process information very differently than I do. Although I formerly practiced law, I'm first and foremost a marketer, and I don't have a typical lawyer's style of communication. I'm more willing to take calculated risks and I don't need every single "i" dotted and "t" crossed before I can be comfortable making a decision.

It became clear to me—*I* was the stupid one. I was presuming a level of knowledge, experience, and insight that they couldn't possibly have. It simply wasn't their job (or skillset) to have it. I was making a rookie mistake.

I began to self-reflect on how I approached the attorneys with my ideas. I would simply walk into the room to meet with the lawyers on the marketing committee, all smiles and confidence, and announce, "I've got a great idea and here it is." I'd just blurt it out and expect them to be able to fill in the picture and do the math, if you will, in their head.

That. Doesn't. Work.

You don't lead with the bottom line and then explain why it's effective. If you start with the conclusion, you've lost them. They will play Devil's Advocate and rip you apart bit by bloody bit, because that's what they do, of course. The ability to identify all the potential problems and pitfalls is often what makes them excellent lawyers. But that's not always the best approach in marketing. So you need to take a different approach.

Instead, you need to unfurl your idea, step by step, in a very logical way that will address their objections before they can actually formulate them. You need to understand how they process information and control the discussion, gradually providing them with the facts and evidence they need. If they control the discussion, it's likely to be, "Yes but what about this? Yes, but what about that? This won't work and here's why...." When that happens, you're back on your heels playing defense, and at that moment, you've lost. Soon after that they'll just say, "No." And once lawyers give you a firm "No," they rarely change their minds.

You may be thinking, "Well, that may have been the case back in the early 1990s, but lawyers' thinking has changed. They've come around. We've shown them the way. They've opened their hearts and they now accept the truth into their lives: Marketing works."

I beg to differ. And, I bet if you really sit back and think about most of your encounters with attorneys at your firm, you'd probably concede that, while they're certainly more accepting of marketing these days and may even understand that it's an important function in running a business, most of them could really take it or leave it. Mostly leave it. There's still resistance. And they approach new ideas with skepticism.

Consequently, this advice—to educate your lawyers about marketing before hitting them with an idea, ad campaign, or novel initiative—remains relevant. You must understand where your lawyers are coming from. Plenty of effective marketing campaigns and tools exist today, of course, but most lawyers don't really look at them. They're not the target audience so they don't see them, or they just don't pay attention. It's not their job. And, most of what they see is bad because most marketing in *every* industry is bad.

It's hard to be great at anything. Many attorneys associate "law firm marketing" with shrieking personal-injury lawyers' billboards and other appallingly over-the-top examples. They may link marketing to ambulance chasers. This type of marketing might be awful, but it's certainly memorable.

This still shapes how many risk-averse lawyers view marketing. Or, as I mentioned in the previous chapter, they opt toward the comfortable clichés—the gavels and scales of justice and courthouses and columns and blahhhhh. You need to change that perception.

Here's how: When you want to get buy-in and launch a marketing project, you need to sit down and write a sales pitch. That is, prepare a detailed presentation, using PowerPoint or some other tool, in which you tell your audience of attorneys how marketing works, what kind of marketing doesn't work, what the competition is doing on the marketing front, what those other firms are doing right and what they're doing wrong, and what you've heard from *them*, the attorneys at your firm, regarding what makes your firm stand out. You want to emphasize that last point, that being distinctive is the key. You must show them good examples and bad examples from law and other industries and help them see the spectrum for themselves. Help them come to the conclusion you want, so they can understand the difference and demand more from their own marketing.

So, you need to teach them about differentiation, and also creativity, marketing budgets, marketing tools and techniques, your firm's position in the marketplace, the evolution of marketing, what you should expect and demand from your marketing, and how it all fits together. Keep in mind that you're planning to say all of this before you get anywhere near unveiling the actual specific ad campaign you've created. You have to lay the educational foundation. You need to be smart about it, humble, too, and don't be afraid to use humor, if you're good at that. And, while you're telling them, you're also showing them. It's important to use a lot of pictures. Attorneys also learn well with examples, quotes, bullet points, citations, and studies.

That's a lot of educating, right? I know it is, so please, understand that preparing this presentation will take you a good chunk of time, perhaps as long as the equivalent of a 40-hour work week. But trust me, it's worth it. You need to have an educated audience or they will shoot you down—for legitimate reasons based on their own experience, which, again, is limited. I've learned that if my team's marketing work is good and our creative strategy is the right one, then I'll get the attorneys to agree. If they don't then either we were flat-out wrong—which usually isn't the case because the materials were based directly on extensive interviews of the firm's lawyers—or I didn't do a sufficient job in teaching them, and that's my fault.

As you're planning this detailed pitch, you've got to know where you want the attorneys to go and you've got to take them there step by step. You need to anticipate where they might object to an element of the marketing campaign and head them off at the pass. You can only do this if you ask yourself, how would a conservative, risk-averse, very smart person perceive this? What are the potential obstacles or objections? And then find a way to fill all of those holes with solid evidence.

You need to quickly flip though screen shots of all their competitors' websites, so they can see how your recommendations will help you stand out. You need to show powerful examples of analogous marketing done by firms they respect and admire in law and other service professions. Help them see that the best firms do the best marketing. You need to teach them the current trends in law firm marketing, supported by hard data from credible sources. Put yourself in your lawyers' shoes and understand that this isn't their world, so it's your job to provide them context. Only after they have a solid understanding of marketing will they be open to your new ideas.

It takes a long time to put these arguments together, just like it does for them when they're litigating a case. But taking the time to make your case is imperative if you want the project to succeed.

Generally for mid-size to large firms, this presentation will first take place before the marketing committee, which is composed mostly of lawyers and marketing staff. You need to get them enthusiastically on board. They will need to become the public evangelists for your project. You'll likely have more time for your presentation with these people and will need to condense it when selling the idea later to the management committee or the entire partnership.

After you write the presentation, with accompanying visuals, you need to practice it. You need to rehearse this presentation over and over. You want to be good—very good. You want to showcase your communication skills and persuade a group of clever, skeptical lawyers who are usually on the other end of the persuasion spectrum. So yes: Practice, practice, practice.

Now, does this really work? Will such a presentation pay dividends, or will your fantastic, inventive marketing creation end up on the cutting-room floor, forcing you to go back to Square One to come up with something watered down and ultimately ineffective, but acceptable for the cautious firm? Let me just say that once I discovered that this is the most-important part of my job, my ideas rarely got rejected. Every marketing project mentioned in this book was launched only after I educated the attorneys. Now my team and I are successful at getting buy-in of our projects 95 percent of the time.

So, yes it does really work.

CHAPTER FIVE

BEST OF BOTH WORLDS:

BRIGHT, BOLD ADS REFLECT
A FIRM'S SIZE & AGILITY

WE'RE SMART. WE'RE OLD. AND WE'RE THE BEST AT EVERYTHING.

UNTIL YOU GRAB THEIR ATTENTION,
THEY CAN'T SEE HOW FABULOUS YOU ARE.

In effective marketing, you need to know what your strengths are. You also must understand that your competitors will try to twist your strength into a weakness. They'll try to turn it upside down and use it against you.

If your firm offers a benefit that others can't copy, consider whether that's something you can use as your differentiator to build your brand around.

Boise-based Hawley Troxell was Idaho's oldest firm. Longevity can be an interesting feature if used correctly, but standing alone, it's rarely enough. Not many prospects exclaim, "If I could just find an *old* firm, *that's* the one I'd hire!"

But you can sometimes use age and history as the hook to convey that you are looking toward the future. It's one possible marketing idea to consider. (Below you can see a couple early ideas for how we considered using it in the firm's marketing, leveraging some late-1800s photos the firm had of its founders working out of a mining camp tent, and a seated founder packing a holstered six-shooter.)

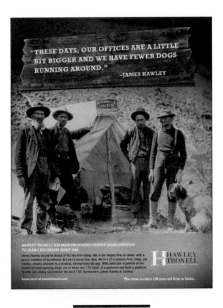

In addition to being its state's oldest firm, Hawley was also Idaho's largest local firm—and size *can* be a strong differentiator. If you're the largest firm in your market, you can easily spin that fact into a narrative of quality, sophistication, more specialty areas, and being the obvious choice for the largest and most-complex matters that require the most specialized expertise. You can assemble larger teams to handle larger matters.

Large is good when you're the big fish, but being the biggest is also a bit dangerous because it can lead to smug complacency. For the largest firms, things seem to be working quite well for them, thank you very much. The 800-pound gorilla in nearly every large city and tiny hamlet tends to avoid taking risks in their marketing. And why should they? They can't imagine a world where they're not the go-to firm, automatically short-listed for the most-interesting work by the most-established clients.

WE'RE SMART. WE'RE OLD. AND WE'RE THE BEST AT EVERYTHING.

And, indeed, Hawley's advertising from this era reflects this complacency.

Those were traditional, staid, even forgettable, and, unfortunately typical of so many promotional efforts in the legal profession.

Here is an example of what they'd been using. Safe, bland, and inoffensive. And, of course, ineffective, but when you're the biggest firm, the message from on high is usually, "First, do no harm." Sure it didn't work, but no one really expected it to. They didn't necessarily even want it to. They just wanted to check the "marketing" box and not upset anyone.

The leaders typically grew up under the kind of risk-averse system reflected in these ads, feeling safe and protected by Hawley's standing as the largest firm around. They most likely earned management seats partially because they didn't rock the boat. This if-it-ain't-broke attitude often creates an opening for hungry smaller firms that have more to prove and more to gain.

When competing against larger opponents, your obvious counter argument is that they're *too* big—a costly, cumbersome battleship whose lawyers have grown fat and lazy. They're not hungry, nimble, or creative.

This was precisely what was happening to Hawley Troxell—the partners at the other firms in and around Boise were working to undermine Hawley's size and strength. I learned early on in my 2011 research that its 45 lawyers were being consistently derided by their smaller competitors. Of course, Hawley would be considered a small firm in most major markets and mid-size in second-tier markets. In Boise, however, it was big.

The Hawley Troxell lawyers knew what the word on the street was about them. "Candidly, we know that our competitors use our size against us," Hawley managing partner Steve Berenter told me back then.

During my interviews with Hawley personnel, I discovered that some of the lawyers and staff members felt the firm was not doing enough to fight back.

It was clear what was happening in Boise. I've seen the same thing in countless other markets—a smaller but more-aggressive competitor moves in to town, or a hungry new firm starts up. Suddenly, those younger firms start doing some innovative, effective marketing, and gradually chip away the legs of your throne. The buzz shifts. You realize that in five years or two years or next year you could be operating in a very different marketplace. You're not growing as fast as your more dynamic competitors.

Hawley was in that situation. Firms were beginning to attract some of the better laterals, which enhanced their standing in the community. They were being perceived as unique and more vibrant. They were shaking up the status quo. While Hawley was still the best-known firm in town, the firm's partners were watching the seeds of change being sown in their own backyard.

Some of the Hawley people told me they felt that the partners needed to up their game.

I agreed completely. Hawley needed a more-aggressive image because they'd been resting on their laurels for a long time. Too long. They'd lost the edge that made them the biggest firm in the first place.

I realized that we had to leverage Hawley's unequivocal strength, namely its size. When you're the biggest firm, you should use that. There are many positive attributes and associations that come with being the biggest. So don't run from that and don't apologize; instead own it and brag about it. We wanted to make clear that they were the biggest—and proud of it.

But—and this is important—we also wanted to paint the picture that, while Hawley maintained all the good traits of being large and resource-deep, they had other good qualities, too. Despite all of the badmouthing about their size from their competitors, they were in fact fast, agile, and nimble.

I wanted Hawley to get adventurous, and reflect who they were with eye-catching images and simple, strong text to convey this best-of-both-worlds, big-yet-nimble approach. My team and I wanted to help them tell their story. By using the type of extensive educational efforts I outlined in the previous chapter, I was able to persuade the partners to embrace the more-aggressive visuals as the heart of a new ad campaign.

As advertising guru David Ogilvy famously wrote, "You can't bore people into buying your product." In law firms, you can't claim to be dynamic and aggressive, then illustrate that with a column and skyline. Remember, with that type of dissonance present in an ad, people will believe what they see, not what you say.

Playing on the positive duality of Hawley's characteristics, we designed magazine ads combining two split-screen photos, one on top of the other to make half-and-half creatures. For example, one depicts the top of an elephant and the bottom half of a sprinting cheetah.

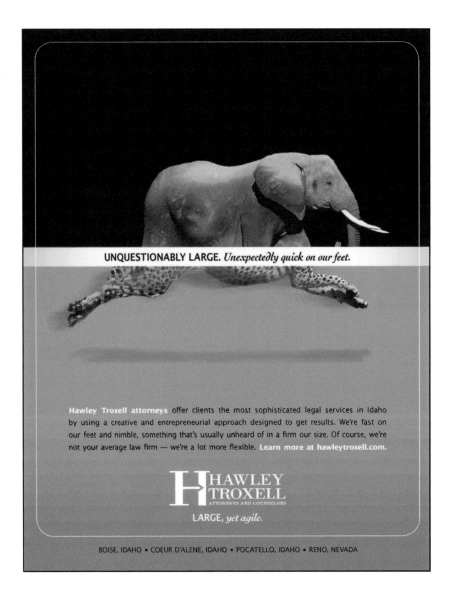

Another shows the upper torso of a brawny football player who has the legs of a figure skater.

In a nod to Idaho wildlife, we devised this diptych of top-half moose and bottom-half antelope.

My favorite presents the face and beefy body of a sumo wrestler who has the legs of a ballerina.

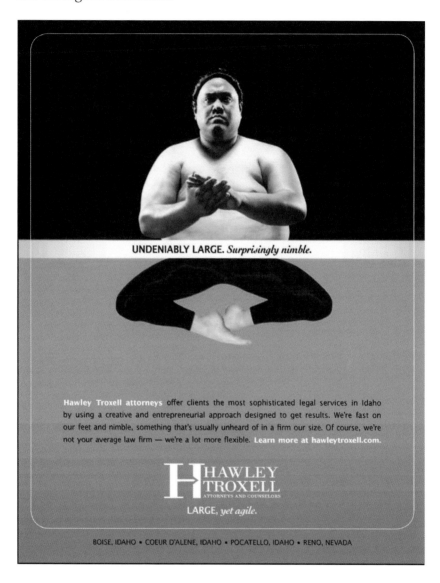

As you can see, separating each pair of images is the thin strip that works well with the composition (that is, it's not distracting), accompanied with the text, "UNQUESTIONABLY LARGE. Unexpectedly quick on our feet." And "UNDENIABLY LARGE. Surprisingly nimble." And the other similar messages. We felt it was important to use Hawley Troxell name and the campaign's tagline, "LARGE, yet agile" under each image.

We've been told—and I don't want to come across as immodest but I'm just telling you what we heard—that quite simply, the ads are fantastic. They're so visually appealing that they're hard not to notice, and the three-word slogan is direct and catchy. Most importantly, the campaign seemed to reflect the way the firm's lawyers thought of themselves. Susan Olson, the executive director, said she wanted "the advertising to match the creativity and dynamic nature of our firm and the way we serve our clients." I wanted that too.

This creative, daring marketing approach is about as far from the firm's previous ads as you can get. The contrast between the old ads and our campaign is pretty striking. With such a grand departure, you'd think there would have been some serious resistance among the senior partners when the firm's marketing staff and my team showed them what we'd been up to and added it to the website home page. Steve Berenter later confided in me that he and some of his folks involved in the process held their collective breath when we rolled the campaign out. I wasn't as worried because I'd given everyone the marketing education presentation.

Still, you never know for sure.

I'm happy to report, however, that the roll out couldn't have gone better. The reaction from the senior partners was absolutely, overwhelmingly positive. And, almost immediately, all of Hawley's people got excited about the campaign. That alone speaks volumes about the firm. By embracing this big change, Hawley attorneys demonstrated that they are creative and open-minded … and nimble.

Of course, all of this would be for naught if it didn't produce results. But it did. In the years following this marketing splash, the firm grew, its revenues and profits rose, and Hawley beefed up lawyer ranks and expanded practices in some of the communities outside of Boise that they serve while still maintaining their grip on the Boise market. Indeed, it's possible and in fact beneficial to be "large yet agile."

CHAPTER SIX

EMBRACE YOUR TRUE CHARACTER:
THE "SMALL BUT MIGHTY" CAMPAIGN

BE HONEST ABOUT YOURSELF AND YOUR CULTURE.
SCREW ANYONE WHO DOESN'T LIKE IT.

Remember when Mom said: "Just be yourself!"?

Well, it turns out, Mom was right.

After you work with hundreds of law firms, you notice some trends, some common themes. One is that, deep down, many small-firm lawyers are insecure. In their marketing, they want to pretend they are something they are not.

They feel like they must apologize for being small. We've heard our clients insist: "Don't say we're small!" It's as though they think if we didn't admit it, their prospects won't notice. No one has ever hired a five- or 25-lawyer firm and was later shocked to find that they didn't have 500 lawyers. *Of course* potential clients are aware of a firm's approximate size.

It's common for small firms to be defensive. You can see this in their website biographies that open by talking about where they *formerly* worked. The not-too-subtle message: "I'm embarrassed to be working at a little firm. Deep down, I'm a big-firm lawyer."

For the biggest cases where there are towering stacks of documents, a great number of bodies may be needed to push all the paper. In these circumstances the client needs a large firm because large firms have enough of these bodies to throw at the problem. In other cases, companies just feel the need to *say* that they hired a big firm; they need the big-firm brand to cover their professional behinds.

These clients will never hire a smaller firm—I don't care who you are. Sophisticated small firms are not ideal for small-dollar disputes, either. But for the 80 percent of cases in the middle, I firmly believe that smaller law firms can be the better option.

Truth be told, there's quite a lot of value in being small, deft, and efficient. You can offer manageable teams, lower hourly rates, less leverage, and more partner time. Clients can hire a big firm and get charged a fortune, or hire a small firm and get charged much less. So boutique firms should use size to their advantage, proudly displaying their value to the world.

The problem with small firms often isn't the quality of their *skills*, but the quality of their *marketing*. With less money to spend, these firms hire lower-quality marketers (if any), and use cheap, template marketing tools. That is a major mistake. If you're the smaller firm, you have more to prove and less margin of error to do that. Therefore, you must do all the "little" things well, particularly marketing. And, as we've seen, marketing is not such a little thing after all.

A boring, ugly website won't harm a large, prestigious law firm and it won't stop their lawyers from getting hired. The giants don't have as much to prove. They're big; their reputations precede them. But a bad website can irreparably damage a small, lesser-known firm. So, I'd argue that small firms not only have to look as good as the big guys, they have to look *better*.

When you're small, you have two philosophical options. You're either (1) small and shoddy, or (2) a high-end boutique. Choose Option 2 every time. The difference is perception. And perception is a function of marketing.

If you're small, don't be embarrassed by it—embrace it. Don't apologize—own it.

In one of our favorite and most-successful campaigns, we helped a firm do just this. Chicago's Novack and Macey is—you guessed it—a small firm. It's a sophisticated, high-end litigation boutique, a big-firm spin-off. They routinely beat up on many large firms in court, when they're not genially co-counseling clients with those same big guys.

Novack and Macey hired us just before they were set to launch their new website. I insisted that they delay the launch—they'd done the process out of order. As in litigation, you develop the message and strategy first, and only then do you identify the persuasive market-ing tools you will use to convey your message. The principal tool, of course, is the website.

The firm hadn't thought of the website in that way, which is very common. Most firms decide they need a new website without consid-ering that it should be their primary messaging tool. In fact, a lot of firms have extremely low expectations for what their website can and should achieve. We still hear that all the time. But in the case of No-vack and Macey, the firm's leadership and marketing team thought about what I'd said and agreed that it made sense.

As I undertook my usual intake process—interviewing the lawyers, getting to know the firm—I learned that Novack and Macey was completely confident in the high quality of their skills. Led by two of Chicago's top trial lawyers, Stephen Novack and Eric Macey, the firm had chosen to be small. That was their foundational strategy and business model. So, getting them to embrace their small size wasn't a problem; they had already done that.

A picture emerged of a friendly, dynamic, tenacious, and intellectu-ally rigorous firm that handled major cases—the full range of busi-ness litigation that boutiques will handle. They co-counseled and co-defended with big firms and also stepped in when there was a conflict with the big firm. Clients who hired them received the full attention of a small, dedicated team in which the retained partner would stay on the matter without passing the client from lawyer to lawyer. And they tried many more cases than the big firms, which gave them a powerful hammer to wield in negotiations.

Novack and Macey understood that they could get hired more often if they could showcase their value. "Yes, they're small, but …" Clients who checked them out were already potentially amenable to hiring a small firm.

At least by embracing the value of "small," Novack and Macey could position themselves as the alternative. In a new-business competition against three larger firms, if you can recast the fundamental decision-making issue as big versus small, you increase your chance of winning the beauty contest. If the prospect can be persuaded to see the value a small firm offers, you win. If they can't, you're going to lose anyway. So don't compete on their terms.

I learned all about the many amazing cases the firm handled, including several representations of large companies in sophisticated, high-dollar litigation. They handled the kinds of cases you would normally expect larger firms to tackle, and they were routinely beating up on large, deep-pocketed firms. They were just better trial lawyers, and they possessed more skills and experience than the other guys. Novack and Macey were punching above their weight.

Our creative team came up with a few ideas and ran them past firm leadership, including their young marketing partners, Monte Mann and John Shonkwiler. One theme in particular resonated strongly and made them say "Oh yeah, that's us." It was entitled "Small but Mighty."

Yes, we all considered the humorous reaction and ribbing that that slogan might evoke. We're always looking for dangerous double entendres and ways that people can poke fun at our clients. Eric Macey was a big part of the marketing revamp process. To his credit, he essentially said, "Oh, grow up. We get the joke; we're fine with it. Let's get it on the table, deal with it, and move past it, because what we want is to be confident. This slogan does convey who we are. Let's not apologize for it. We want you all out there using this to tell our story."

His instinct proved to be correct. The campaign turned out to be one of the most popular we've ever done, and it's one people remember to this day.

We created ads featuring pictures of small things in nature that packed a disproportionately powerful wallop. In order to engage the entire firm in the process, we decided to run a little competition, challenging firm lawyers and staffers to do their own research and come up with their own small-but-mighty images, offering prizes for any examples we picked, to supplement our originals.

WE'RE SMART. WE'RE OLD. AND WE'RE THE BEST AT EVERYTHING.

These examples included the pea-sized Tepín pepper, one of the hottest peppers in the world,

the 4-inch rhino beetle, which can carry 850 times its own weight,

and the tiny Poison Dart Frog, which can kill you if you touch its beautiful, colorful skin.

These images appeared in an integrated campaign which included a logo and identity materials, the "Small but Mighty" tag line, website, print ads, firm brochure, giveaways, and direct mailers.

At the launch party, the valiant John Shonkwiler agreed to take one for the team, actually *eating* one of the hot peppers on camera to help generate a feature story in the *Chicago Daily Law Bulletin*. Red-faced and sweating, John survived the fiery blast and the article made the front page.

To help keep the law firm in the top of their targets' minds we later sent small, private-labeled packets of Tepín peppers to 2,500 members of our mailing list (complete with hazmat warnings), which created a great buzz. A decade later, we still occasionally see our pepper packets on referring lawyers' credenzas. We also direct-mailed tiny inch-high brochures and miniscule magnifying glasses that were fitted into miniature leather dolls' briefcases. And, we found realistic plastic poison dart frogs, fastened them to the tiny brochures, and placed them around the firm, including in a glass bowl in the lobby.

After all, who can resist a free plastic poison dart frog?

Within 18 months of the launch of the campaign, the firm had grown by 40 percent. Still small, just not quite *as* small. It also received an international award for creative and effective marketing.

The campaign ran successfully for many years, first in print, then online. After drastically increasing the firm's name recognition and solidifying its stellar reputation, we turned to a different prong of the marketing campaign. It was time to focus on increasing referrals by marketing directly to the Chicago-area legal community.

Most litigation boutiques receive a sizable amount of their work through referrals from other law firms. We wanted to remind target firms that not only is Novack and Macey a highly skilled, small-but-mighty firm, but that it should be the first name that comes to mind when a referral is needed. This was an extension of their message, aimed squarely at lawyers.

Our solution was to turn the firm name into a verb. To "Novack and Macey" something would mean to "send a litigation referral." Ads that included the tagline "We Novack and Macey'd it" were a memorable way to reinforce the firm name while also explaining clearly the behavior we wanted from the readers.

This campaign also produced successful results as the firm kept its name in front of its targets and saw their referrals rise.

The "Small but Mighty" marketing campaign speaks to the value of accepting yourself for who you are as a firm. Highlight your strengths about that identity and shout your message clearly, creatively, and loudly out into the world.

CHAPTER SEVEN

BLAZE NEW TRAILS:
FIRST-EVER SERVICE GUARANTEE

IF YOU WANT TO ACHIEVE BETTER RESULTS, YOU MUST DO SOMETHING *DIFFERENT.*

If they made movies about law firm marketing campaigns in the style of classic sports movies, *Service Guarantee: The Coffield Ungaretti & Harris Story* would be the equivalent of *Rocky, Hoosiers,* and *Field of Dreams* rolled into one.

The plot: The 1989 recession hits. The real estate market tanks. Firms across the country fire their real estate lawyers. The Chicago firm of Coffield Ungaretti & Harris gets knocked around. Its leading real estate practice suffers. The struggling firm quickly drops from 100 lawyers to 60. For some reason, the media turns Coffield Ungaretti into the highly publicized poster child for Chicago law firm downsizing. Speculation runs rampant that the firm is teetering on the edge and in danger of folding. And, in fact, it is.

The partners vote to tighten their belts and hang on, enabling the firm to recover well enough in a flat national market. It's now five years later, 1994. Coffield Ungaretti hasn't grown, but they've stayed stable at 60 lawyers. They're quietly doing fine. Not great, but neither is anyone else during those lean years. Of course, no editor wants to write a feature story about a firm doing "fine," so the lagging reputation lingers.

Wary prospects are reluctant to send their business to a tarnished firm that they heard might fold soon. Clients come and go. The firm has always grown by hiring laterals, but they have a staggering 25 percent annual attorney turnover, that is, literally *half* the firm turns over every two years, including partners, and constantly hiring and replacing lawyers is extremely inefficient. The best lateral hires don't care to join a firm that, last they heard, was in grave danger.

The firm's primary asset is a dynamic young marketing committee whose members, Dennis Gallitano, Gwen Carroll, and Kevin Flynn, are ready to shake things up. They don't know exactly what to do, but they know they need to do something drastic to change Coffield Ungaretti's fortunes. They try to hire me away from my marketing job at Winston & Strawn because they heard that I might be the guy who could help. I'm reluctant at first, because I too had heard that they were in danger of collapse. But after enough wining and dining, including showing me the actual revenue numbers, it becomes clear to me that they're doing fine. Unfortunately, the negative reputation continues to linger. It's killing them. I decide to join the firm.

The problem with Coffield Ungaretti isn't quality, it's perception. And again, perception is a function of marketing. *Perception* we can fix. *Reputation* we can change. Building a strong, positive reputation is hard; overcoming a negative one is even harder. You can't just say, "We don't suck any more!" and expect people to believe you.

We need something bold, something new and eye-catching. We need to change the narrative. We need to create a bright shiny object to distract people from the negative perception they'd held for five years and show them something entirely different. We need to grab the marketplace by the lapels and *shake* it.

We need to make Coffield Ungaretti the coolest firm in town. But *how?*

* * *

Here's a little more backstory to set the scene:

In the early- and mid-90s, law firm marketing was still in its infancy. At Coffield Ungaretti, we were extremely fortunate to have a business-oriented managing partner who was willing to take a calculated risk for a program he believed in. We also had a talented internal marketing team, as well as the aforementioned aggressive and influential marketing committee. These factors combined to position the firm exceptionally well to try something unique—something to make a splash. In such an atmosphere it was relatively easy for me to educate the partnership through strategic presentations, and then get their approval and enthusiastic participation.

The legal community's perception of Coffield Ungaretti had lagged far behind the firm's true revitalization. We needed to create a new narrative. We wanted to bring external opinion of the firm in line with the reality of skilled attorneys offering top-notch legal and client services. We needed the entire legal community to collectively say, "Huh, I didn't know that about Coffield Ungaretti! Wow!"

At that time, a shift was occurring in the atmosphere surrounding the legal landscape. In-house lawyers were just beginning to realize that they held the power in the attorney-client relationship. They were mad as hell at their perceived mistreatment by firms, and were starting to flex their muscles, drafting stern standards for how they expected to be treated by outside counsel. They were increasing their demands for client service, in areas including communication, responsiveness, accessibility, timeliness, and billing. There seemed to be an opening for a firm willing to not just defensively accept their harsh terms, but graciously offer them.

I extensively researched customer service strategies, learning that guarantees work across industries. Not only do clients like and appreciate them, they work as a direct incentive to businesses to continually improve service. A guarantee seemed like the key to turning Coffield Ungaretti's fortunes around.

Although it looked risky at the time, our guarantee idea was based on the existing reality of realization rates. Clients are going to pay you what they think they're getting value for anyway. Law firms discount their services all the time for clients who don't think they're receiving an appropriate level of value. That is, if they don't think they got a dollar's worth of value out of the dollar you billed them, they ain't paying you the whole dollar. And if you try to squeeze them for a few cents more, they might pay it, but they'll resent it. And you. And they'll remember.

A wealth of research shows that the longer an organization can keep its clients, the more profitable they become. Increased retention increases revenue. If you can find out what your clients think of your performance, you have a much better chance of making adjustments and retaining their business.

At that time, client surveys were becoming popular as a means to gain insight into clients' thoughts on law firm performance. The problem was they were typically "end of matter" surveys presented after the fact. If the client said "we didn't like the associate you put on our matter," or "your bills were too confusing," or any of the other countless service critiques or complaints they could make, it was too late to do anything about it. They were upset and weren't likely to hire us again. I wanted them to let us know of any service irregularities at the time they occurred, so we could still fix the problem. We decided to make our guarantee ongoing and proactive, not reactive.

We also conducted proprietary market research that disclosed that inadequate communication caused most problems in attorney-client relationships. Dissatisfied clients won't hesitate to leave, either—80 percent take their business elsewhere. We pledged that any problems that arose would be detected "promptly" and repaired to the client's satisfaction. In effect we just took responsibility for any miscommunications and offered to make adjustments—the adjustments the firm was likely to make anyway.

This promise was no tacky "money-back" guarantee, however. That crass commercial attitude would have undermined a key principle: Write-offs don't keep clients satisfied. What does make them happy is building relationships and having their service needs met. Succeeding with these basics lays the groundwork for boosting firm profits. Client focus groups helped us identify the best language to convey the firm's commitment to the positive, integrity-filled behavior that clients desire, including a resolve to provide the finest technical skills.

Writing the guarantee took a great deal of finesse. We wanted to provide an incentive for clients to identify problems early on. We wanted to know if clients were feeling that a matter wasn't being handled in the best way. Yet, we still had to compartmentalize the guarantee somewhat because it simply couldn't be an open-ended, indefinite, unlimited offer. I imagined the lawyers' protests: "Hold on. What if 10 years into a big antitrust case a client suddenly claims a nagging sense of dissatisfaction and demands that we return $10 million in fees?" Of course none of us wanted to enable a scenario like that.

So, I needed to draft a guarantee that subtly prohibited that type of behavior. It needed to include a good-faith aspect for both sides without appearing to be nitpicking. Naturally with any guarantee, skeptical clients are going to first scan the bottom of the page for the asterisk, and a guarantee with fine print really is no guarantee at all. I knew it had to exclude undermining language—but it still needed some subtle or implied qualifiers.

I shaped the guarantee's language to reinforce and reward the close communication that "promptly" identifies hidden problems, aiming to nip issues in the bud by resolving them before they grow and fester. Such an approach produces hard evidence of the firm's service and, indirectly, of its technical skills. This course of action gets much better results than simply making an unsubstantiated pablum "good service" declaration.

All this would have been to no avail had the guarantee been an empty public relations stunt. It was, in fact, a legally binding client contract—a firm-wide mission statement with razor-sharp teeth. Coffield Ungaretti was the first law firm to offer this type of pledge, and it quickly formed a differentiated identity for the firm. The bold move changed the perception that this was a firm in financial dire straits. That made all the difference.

The five-sentence statement formed the nucleus of Coffield Ungaretti's strategic business and marketing program to improve and publicize client service and retention, decrease attorney attrition, grow strategically, and, of course, to increase revenues and profits.

We used both vigorous advertising and media relations to spread this message, and accompanied the guarantee campaign with several support strategies. Reasoning that we could gain significant publicity by being the first firm to offer such a guarantee, we launched an aggressive push to actively court the media. When you have an interesting story, it's not that hard to persuade publications to write about it. Soon dozens of resulting positive feature stories appeared in major outlets and amplified our message around the world.

Our team also engaged in targeted advertising. In those days local law firms did very little creative promotion. We sought to take advantage of this gap by leveraging our message and boosting our image among our local business and legal community audiences. We also worked with an outside ad agency to develop a daring-but-corporate-looking campaign and placed these ads in local edition of *The Wall Street Journal*, *Crain's Chicago Business*, and several Chicago-area and selected national legal periodicals.

By design, we made the ad to look like the Declaration of Independence and all the partners signed it. We thought it was visually very powerful. What do you think?

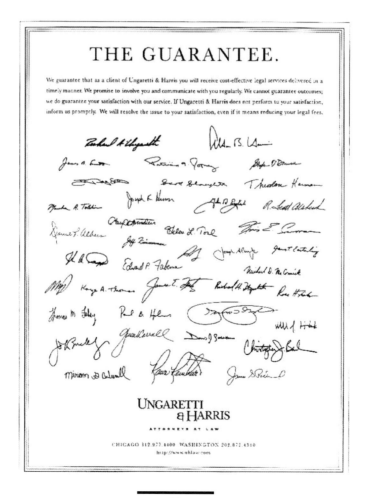

Here's what our pledge said:

> We guarantee that as a client of Coffield Ungaretti & Harris, you will receive cost-effective legal services delivered in a timely manner. We promise to involve you and communicate with you. We cannot guarantee outcomes; we do guarantee your satisfaction with our service. If Coffield Ungaretti & Harris does not perform to your satisfaction, inform us promptly. We will resolve the issue to your satisfaction, even if it means reducing your legal fees.

As we've seen, all our efforts paid off handsomely. The results speak for themselves:

- In just one year, during a stagnant legal market and following five flat years:
  - Revenues jumped 50 percent, compared to the profession's 2 percent average growth.
  - We grew in size by 50 percent, from 60 to 95 attorneys, compared to the profession's 2 percent average, ranking us among the nation's 10 fastest-growing firms.
  - Attorney retention increased 400 percent, to just half the profession's average attorney turnover. The firm lost no partners and none of the few departing associates went to competing firms for two straight years. The grass was suddenly greener here, so why would anyone volunteer to leave?
  - Client retention increased significantly.
- Dozens of positive feature articles were written about the firm, from The New York Times and Chicago Tribune to The American Lawyer and the ABA Journal. The firm was also the subject of a three-minute "Special Report" on the local ABC-TV affiliate news and numerous radio shows.
- Success in new-business competitions increased from 15 percent to 50 percent, generating millions of dollars in fees.
- We attracted many high-quality lateral hires.
- The guarantee stood for 20 years, until the firm (later

renamed Ungaretti & Harris) was merged in 2015 into Nixon Peabody.

* * *

Now, back to our movie.

The tale of the Coffield Ungaretti "Written Service Guarantee" is an example of how marketing can help to drastically improve law firm's fortunes. It also exemplifies the idea that sometimes—often?—you must push the proverbial envelope.

And, what's a classic movie without a good, old-fashioned newspaper montage of spinning headlines to summarize events?

"Law Firm Develops First Written Service Guarantee"
… "Coffield Ungaretti Revenue Up Sharply"
… "Firm Undergoes Major Growth Spurt"
… "Client Retention Soars"
… "Attorney Retention Quadruples"
… "Firm Develop Stellar National Reputation
for Groundbreaking Client Service"

Fifteen years after the success of Coffield's guarantee, Fishman Marketing rebranded a terrific St. Louis law firm, Sandberg Phoenix & von Gontaard. While interviewing its lawyers, I discovered that *they* might have actually been the first firm to offer some sort of written service guarantee, but they never made a big deal out of it. So, while it helped continuously improve their first-rate client service, it didn't benefit their external marketing or reputation. Coffield Ungaretti got all the plaudits for being first.

Sandberg Phoenix might not have been seen as the first, but we could still make them the first in their local market, which can be both effective and lucrative. We developed an advertising and marketing campaign designed around the idea of how unlikely it would be for a law firm to offer such a service guarantee, using metaphors for incredulity like pigs flying, money growing on trees, lightning striking twice, and ... the Chicago Cubs winning the World Series, which, at the time, seemed impossible. (By the way, thank you, 2016 Cubs! ... But that's another movie.)

Did marketing a service guarantee work for them too?

Of course it did.

Roll credits.

& CHAPTER EIGHT

FIRST IMPRESSIONS:
LOGOS MAKE THE WORLD GO 'ROUND

THEY WON'T MAKE YOU MONEY, BUT THESE LITTLE PIECES OF ART *DO* MATTER.

Okay, that may be a tad overstated. Actually, it might be a grand exaggeration but nonetheless logos are important—and they mean more to some people than others.

A good logo is an essential part of your firm's marketing strategy. Even though logos don't necessarily win or lose you clients, they often set a first impression. Whether on your website or a business card, a logo is one of the first things people experience about your firm at a crucial time, when they're searching for clues about what kind of quality is attached to it. Whereas a slapdash logo makes your firm look substandard, an outstanding , professionally designed logo creates an impressive, professional tone. So yes, logos matter, a lot, which is why I want to spend more than a few pages on this subject.

Logos convey critical information about who you are. In effect, they're little pieces of artwork that summarize and encapsulate the entire firm and its culture with a few words, a color, and perhaps an image. But lawyers often don't give logo design the respect it deserves. *They look so small and simple—how tricky can it be, really, to come up with one of those things? Pick a standard Word font, bold or italicize part of the name, center it, then pick a color. That's it.*

Well, that's *not* it. Crafting a *good* logo is actually quite a complicated process.

Think about some of the iconic logos we encounter every day, like Nike's swoosh, McDonald's golden arches, or Target's concentric circles. They instantly and distinctively identify their institutions. One glance at the nuance and connection of these logos tells you that they were not an afterthought that someone's kid did on their Mac or cooked up at Kinko's. They show that great organizations invest time and money in these sorts of things because *they matter*. While it's unlikely any law firm logo will ever be as well-known as those company marks, law firms categorically need professional designers to craft their logos.

Because logos are small works of art, everybody has an opinion about them. Lawyers are entitled to their own opinions, of course (even if they're uneducated opinions). They know what they like, even though they don't know exactly why. What they like may be awful from a professional designer's perspective, but they still like it.

Many attorneys seem to like having initials next to their logo. Often they want the initials in a box. They like boxes. Initials and boxes just look *design-y* to some of them. And they have their former art history-major spouse weighing in with *their* opinions, as well. (We once had a client who proclaimed, "I showed the logo to my wife. She took some art classes in high school, and she said 'law firms shouldn't use blue.'" That was all the evidence he needed. He insisted we select a new color. True story.)

So, all these strong-but-uneducated opinions on logos mean three things: 1) Surprise! Egos become entwined in the logo-choosing process. 2) Selecting a new logo can ignite a firm-wide battle if it's not done carefully. 3) Like in so many other marketing-related areas, lawyers need to be educated about logos and design before they should be asked to make a good decision.

NOTHING BUT THE TRUTH & NOTHING PERSONAL

In many rebranding campaigns, a key decision must be made before we can begin to tackle the logo: which names will make it onto the logo, and how prominently they'll be displayed. Tackling this step requires a little sublimating of egos—never an easy task in most law firm environments.

I come at it from the objective outsider's position. I let them know I don't have a dog in the fight—"I'm just the marketing guy and I'm going to tell you the truth as I see it." I don't refer to the names as "names." Instead, I call them "words." This subtly lets them know that it's not about the actual people or their relative value. In a firm name some of the partners may be dead, still practicing, big rainmakers, insecure, beloved, or controversial; it's usually a mix. You have to show them that the decision is not about who is more important; it's just about marketing. Nothing personal.

I always make it very clear that we're not changing the *name* of the firm; we're just changing the *logo*. Unless you have a truly awful, impossible-to-spell-or-pronounce firm name, use your firm's "street name"—the one everybody calls it anyway. Deep down, your lawyers know what that is.

I show lawyers examples of firms that have followed this rule, often using the mighty New York-based global giant Skadden, Arps, Meager, & Flom as a prime example. For many years, Joe Flom was the managing partner and the most important lawyer at the firm, and yet his name came last. Under his leadership, the firm changed its logo to read "Skadden." That's it. Just "Skadden." Why? For the obvious reasons—that's what everybody called them. Also, highlighting that one name made for a more powerful logo.

As Harry Beckwith wrote in *What Clients Love*, "The human brain rejects names of more than four syllables, and abbreviates them. The brain turned Harley Davidson into Harley… Shorter names can be larger, making their name more familiar. Small names act bigger."

The New Orleans firm Lugenbuhl, Wheaton, Peck, Rankin & Hubbard is another case in point. Changing the logo to prominently feature "Lugenbuhl," with the full firm name written in small type at the bottom, does not in any way suggest that Mr. Lugenbuhl was a better person or a smarter lawyer or otherwise more valuable than the four other name partners. It's just that his name came first, and fortunately his moniker is strong, unique, and memorable—a great name to use.

There's no danger that anyone will confuse that firm with another with a similar name. No one in New Orleans ever said, "Which Lugenbuhl firm do you mean?" Managing partner S. Rodger Wheaton, the second name on the list, understood that emphasizing "Lugenbuhl" was a sound decision, and he selflessly advocated for that strategy within the firm.

To seal the deal in my pitch presentations, I often juxtapose the current and redesigned logos in actual usage, for example, showing the attendees how the new logo would look on a t-shirt or hat. It's hard to argue that the "before" version here works better.

Now, a word about initials. Unless your firm is DLA Piper or perhaps K&L Gates, stay away from them on logos and websites and everywhere else. Nobody refers to a firm by its initials, and with rare exception, a random collection of initials is nonsensical, awkward, and forgettable.

In one of my favorite marketing books, *Positioning: The Battle for Your Mind*, Al Reis and Jack Trout make the case that "To be well-known, you've got to avoid using initials. Once you get to the top, once you are well known, *then* initials can be used without ambiguity." The point is that most of the prominent organizations that use initials (for example GE, GM, KPMG, IBM, AT&T, FBI, CIA, NBC, CBS, *etc.*) started out with a cumbersome name that their customers eventually abbreviated for their own convenience. Law firms rarely have analogous experiences.

Remember, just because internally you refer to your firm by its initials doesn't mean that anyone else does. I started practicing law at

Pedersen & Houpt, which we often called "P&H." But that was only with our own people; using it outside of the firm would have been confusing.

I often switch things up for firms, by, for example changing their one-line logo to a two-line logo. The choice of one line or two lines can be a delicate one, with power implications. *"I don't want my name smaller than that partner's,"* or *"I don't want my name alone on the top line because I don't want that guy to think I'm saying I'm more important than he is."*

To talk them out of their natural resistance you have to show them the shape that you'll most typically be using the logo in, and how that helps set it apart from the pack. They can see with their own eyes that your alterations really did improve the visual punch. It's the same width, it doesn't take up any more space, but in the common movie-screen aspect-ratio that they're accustomed to, a two-line logo generally works much better than a one-line logo—unless it's embossed on a pencil.

Now let's look at it from a distance. Let's see how it looks if we were to put it on a baseball cap or t-shirt. Let's talk ampersands. Let's talk weighted to the left vs. weighted to the right vs. centered. Let's look at it in a box. Do you see that this *is not as good as* that?

Once they can see for themselves what pops, then you've got them.

We recently rebranded 100-lawyer Galloway, Johnson, Tompkins, Burr & Smith, which had been using a "giant initials"-style logo. It's admittedly an egalitarian approach, intended to show that all of the firm's founders are equally important. Unfortunately, from a marketing perspective, big bold initials shrink the size of the firm name—the very thing we want prospects to remember. Our recommendation was to change the logo to emphasize "Galloway," a providentially short, simple, strong, and easy to spell name. If the goal is simple communication, to help people identify and remember the firm name, one strong name tends to work better than a random collection of initials. The contrast is pretty obvious.

BEFORE

GALLOWAY
JOHNSON
TOMPKINS
BURR AND
SMITH

A Professional Law Corporation

AFTER

GALLOWAY

Galloway Johnson Tompkins Burr & Smith

It pays to be selective when showing lawyers logo choices. For example, if you show them four different attractive versions, then the room will divide roughly into quarters and you'll have created a fight for yourself. Even if the logo that "wins" is terrific, it's not the one that three-fourths of the lawyers in the room picked, and because their preferred logo didn't make the cut, they're disappointed, and they'll never love the new logo.

On the other hand, if you're careful in how you sell them on the one finalist logo, if you first educate them about the merits of that design, you can help them feel great about that single option.

LET'S TALK ABOUT COLOR

Lawyers typically aren't known for their daring fashion-forward sense. They tend to like safe, conservative colors like burgundy, navy blue, or pine green. Most have no reason to consider that law firm logo colors have been changing. Morgan Lewis used orange before many would dare and recently changed to a rich purple. Linklaters has used pink, Hogan Lovells chartreuse, and Littler a bright green and blue.

Even Big Four accounting firms use vibrant colors. EY uses a bright yellow, Deloitte uses blue with a lime green dot, and PWC uses a kaleidoscope of reds, oranges, and pink. Using these colors can be audacious, but it's difficult to credibly claim you're bold and confident and fresh and new when your logo is navy blue or maroon.

Consider that many lawyers consider their logo to be the tangible encapsulation of their entire legal career. It's right there every time they pull out their business card. They tend to be very insecure about these kinds of image issues. … *I had three years of law school and many years of practice. I'm a leader in the industry. I'm not pink! Pink is for little girls.*

I've marveled at firms that do use bright purples and pinks and similar colors and also get their lawyers to buy into it. Even the oldest, most conservative partners have to reach into their wallets and hand out those cards—pink logo and all. To have those attorneys get on board with the new look and still feel good about themselves and their career is challenging. Usually, you have to hear a slew of pro- and con-arguments about color choices:

The following are all actual marketing committee comments:
> *Lawyers shouldn't be orange!*
> *Red is the color of bankruptcy—I don't want to be in the red!*
> *Let's use green; green is money! … No, green is envy!*
> *I want our logo to match your blue suit. Give me your jacket!*

Even college rivalries come into play. *Some of our lawyers went to Auburn. We can't use red—that's Alabama's color!*

Everyone has an opinion about colors, but few have the skills or training to understand the nuances. Of course, we make color decisions every day, so the issues seems easy to the layperson. I've also heard:
> *We just redecorated our kitchen, so I'm a bit of a color expert, and I think…*

This color looks different on my laptop. We need a color that doesn't change.

Yes, the arguments involving color decisions really can get this ridiculous. But educating lawyers step by step about why a particular color makes sense will usually result in a good outcome and a fresh new look for the firm. I show lawyers dozens of other firm logos to demonstrate that it's okay not to be navy blue, and that even powerful, conservative, global firms can use bright colors.

Fisher Phillips is one of the nation's largest labor and employment firms, with 350+ skilled lawyers across 33 offices. Growing fast, they needed to differentiate themselves from the other national boutiques. We underscored their leadership with a bold new "On the Front Lines of Workplace Law" brand, including designing a daring new three-dimensional logo in a vibrant red, dropping the ampersand, and creating a look that stood out in stark contrast to their staid competitors.

BEFORE

AFTER

A major color change, however, isn't always the correct tactic. Sometimes we'll conclude that so much is getting redone in a firm-wide rebrand that switching the logo color is just going to put people over the edge. So we'll tell them: "Hey, let's stay with a blue—not royal or navy blue, though. Let's modernize it but stay in the blue family so it doesn't feel as jarring."

In many cases, when we add just a little bit of color in the right place, we can truly transform a design. The emblem of Florida's Bryant, Miller, Olive is a good example. The firm liked its logo, but it consisted of three words on one line, and that was just too long. To redesign a logo, you have to consider the expense, because you're also going to be redesigning the business cards, the letterhead, and all the other places that it's used—even all the metal signage on the elevator banks.

We found a way to keep the typeface but make the shape work better by stacking the names on three lines instead of one. We kept the main color black but changed the dot in the i in "Olive" to olive green, to support the olive-themed branding campaign. It was fairly subtle, but that little green dot makes all the difference, as you can see.

BEFORE

Bryant ▪ Miller ▪ Olive
ATTORNEYS AT LAW

AFTER

Bryant
Miller
Olive
ATTORNEYS AT LAW

A BALANCING ACT

Balance is another key factor in logo design. While it might not be as obvious at first glance as color—you might not consciously notice it if you're not the designer—a well-balanced logo just *feels* right. It feels like quality.

When we helped full-service Moffatt Thomas redesign their logo, we started with the message. We wanted to convey leadership, confidence, strength, and stability, while giving the firm more fresh and modern representation. The two words are similarly sized, and by shifting "Moffatt" to the right, we got a nice opportunity to create a sense of equilibrium by lining up the two o's, and the two f's with the m, and the two offset a's to create an appealing slant. The slight diagonal also makes the logo more interesting and easier to read, a characteristic particularly important for words in all capitals, which are generally harder to read than lower-case letters.

We kept a blue color for historic continuity, but updated its tone. The result is an appealing logo that skillfully portrays Moffatt Thomas's message:

BEFORE

Moffatt Thomas

MOFFATT THOMAS BARRETT ROCK & FIELDS, CHTD.

AFTER

MOFFATT THOMAS

IMAGERY HELPS PAINT THE PORTRAIT

Sometimes a little creative imagery is all it takes to make a logo go from dull to unforgettable.

In 2015, Atlanta's Constangy Brooks & Smith saw an opportunity to take the lead in diversity by simultaneously hiring dozens of skilled lawyers nationwide at once. The firm decided to add one prominent lawyer to the firm name.

We created a logo for the renamed firm to help them portray a message of inclusion and diversity and to illustrate their new slogan, "A Wider Lens on Workplace Law." The chosen logo effectively conveys this, with an iris-shape suggesting a camera lens:

BEFORE

AFTER

With the Tucson, AZ firm of Waterfall, Economidis, Caldwell, Hanshaw & Villamana, PC, we spotted a branding opportunity using the firm's memorable first name. "Waterfall" is a positive word, connoting strength, confidence, and nature. We built the marketing platform using dramatic photos of waterfalls, and headlines that describe their skills and professionalism. We overhauled the equally sized logo, emphasizing "Waterfall" and designing the W to create a sense of movement. This strong message is supported by an equally strong tag line, "As Powerful as Our Name."

BEFORE

AFTER

The logo we designed for the firm of Goldberg Simpson was intended to help the firm shake things up—and we think it certainly did just that. This Louisville, KY partnership is a dynamic and creative firm, with market leadership in a wide variety of commercial and consumer-oriented practice areas. Its marketing materials, however, had historically conveyed a conservative message that was at odds with its energy, diversity, and innovation.

We came up with "A law firm that really moves" campaign which featured a new logo—or, really, new logos, plural—that sport silhouettes of objects in motion, including a soaring jet, a running man, a pirouetting ballerina, a racing motorcycle, a streaking arrow, a high-flying Kentucky Wildcat jump shooter, and yes, a galloping Bluegrass-country thoroughbred, inserted (one per logo, mind you) over the firm's name.

GOLDBERG SIMPSON
A Law Firm that Really *Moves.*™

GOLDBERG SIMPSON
A Law Firm that Really *Moves.*™

GOLDBERG SIMPSON
A Law Firm that Really *Moves.*™

Our new favorite logo is one we designed for Albany-based Cooper Erving & Savage, a 230-year-old firm, the second-oldest law firm in the United States. Dating to 1785, the firm's archive boasts legal documents including a real estate deed signed by a local Native American chief with a pictogram of a turtle. We used that graphic in their logo, to support the firm's history-oriented brand message. You can read more about Cooper Erving and its logo, under the "History" case study.

BEFORE

Cooper Erving & Savage LLP
Protecting Our Clients' Rights Since 1813

AFTER

COOPER ERVING

The point is, start by understanding your story and your strategy, then see if you need to revise your logo to reinforce that message.

Congratulations, you've made it to the end of Part One. I hope I've persuaded you that there's a sizable competitive advantage to standing out in your chosen market. The next step is determining how to apply these branding concepts to your firm and its unique situation.

It's time for introspection and analysis. Where are you in your market? What's your strategic challenge? What would you like to be known for? Do you need to fix a negative perception or spread the word about something you're proud of or especially good at? What is unique about you, your style, personality, culture, or practice mix? Are there any industries in which you have particular strength or expertise?

CONCLUSION: PART ONE

So that's the basic background; I hope it makes sense and spurs you to action. It can be hard to be objective about your firm, but if you conduct the internal investigation discussed above, if you interview your own lawyers in a systematic way, you can usually find a common thread that binds everyone together and creates your distinctive culture.

Listen for common words the lawyers use when discussing their practices and the firm, and always probe deeper. Always ask, "Tell me more about that." It's there, you must simply uncover it.

Are your lawyers more caring, creative, efficient, experienced, faster, friendlier, or better listeners? Are you a high-end boutique or offer more full-service practices? Do you offer lower prices or more value? Are you problem solvers, unusually responsive, or more service oriented? Are you tougher, do you understand clients' industries, or take more time to understand their businesses?

These are just some of the concepts around which you can build your brand. But you can't be all of them. Pick one word or direction, and seek to *own* that idea in your market.

PART TWO

CASE STUDIES

CASE STUDIES

Every person in a creative field keeps an "Ideas" file, full of innovative materials that can spur their imagination. There are only so many solutions to any particular challenge, and it can be helpful to see how others have addressed it in the past. It can create the spark of inspiration that can get you unstuck.

After working on the creative side of law firm marketing for 25 years, we've helped solve hundreds of different problems for firms, many of which fall into distinct categories.

What do you do when you are a small firm up against larger competitors, are in a unique geography, or have a tricky name? What are some promotional options when your firm has an interesting history, or a leading industry or practice group? How do you leverage a strong win record or an unusual culture?

The following pages are representative examples of how we've addressed dozens of these types of issues for law firms large and small. Consider them your own "Ideas" file—a starting point for how you might solve your own unique marketing problems. We've detailed some of the project's background, to provide some insight into how we came to the recommended solution.

I hope they're helpful.

If you'd ever like to discuss your firm's own unique challenges, feel free to contact me directly at ross@fishmanmarketing.com or +1.847.432.3546.

PRACTICE-SPECIFIC

FAMILY LAW:
MACLEAN FAMILY LAW GROUP

Family law and trust & estate law require a delicate touch. That goes for marketing these specialties as well as handling clients.

Family law can get *personal*. And messy. Lawyers often become intimately acquainted with things like family secrets, messy divorces, simmering tensions among relatives, sibling rivalries, long-held grudges, affairs, addictions, squandered fortunes, businesses run into the ground by wayward children or grandchildren. The list goes on. Even in families that don't consider themselves dysfunctional, trouble can arise. Money has a way of doing that.

Lawyers handling family law matters need discretion, compassion, and good people skills. Effective marketing for these practices should not deny the sensitive nature of the issues being hashed out by clients and attorneys.

We followed this philosophy when we went to work on a marketing campaign for a new British Columbia firm. After spending several years in a prominent Vancouver family law partnership, Lorne MacLean left to found his own firm and pursue a more upscale client base. The MacLean Family Law Group had the skills to justify the new focus, but needed to create a brand appropriate for this sophisticated audience. And with all the expenses inherent in launching a new firm, they needed to make a big impact on a small budget.

The dynamic new organization enlisted Fishman Marketing to develop a marketing program to target this community. Fortunately, firm leader MacLean is an especially creative and dynamic senior partner, and he was willing to take calculated risks to generate the buzz he needed to encourage the lawyer referrals that were the primary source of his business.

WE'RE SMART. WE'RE OLD. AND WE'RE THE BEST AT EVERYTHING.

One highly visible tool was our print ad campaign, which used elegant black and white wedding photos of happy couples in love. The accompanying text is a series of heartbreaking, first-person narratives describing the decline of the relationship that led to the divorces. It shows the raw, human, emotional side of the practice. But instead of talking about the law firm, it put the reader in the shoes of the couple. That's a powerful strategy.

The graceful design resembles an elegant wedding invitation, which stood in stark contrast to the cluttered, heavy-handed design of many slapdash telephone-directory legal advertisements then competing for the family law market.

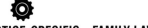

Simultaneously we launched a bold and visually striking awareness and name-recognition campaign designed to generate buzz and referrals from local Vancouver lawyers. The photographic image is a wedding cake, with the bride figurine on the top tier. She is alone, gazing forlornly at the trail of tiny footsteps leading away from her and off the cake. The image instantly conveys "divorce," and contrasts the happiness of the wedding with the poignant result.

We didn't feel that divorce clients are looking for funny lawyers, and so this wasn't aimed directly at the clients. And when you need to break thought the clutter and build visibility on a small budget, it helps to go big. Invest more on the creative side with bolder branding, and you achieve results more quickly and cost-effectively.

The moving but practical tag line reads: "We can't protect your heart. But we can protect your rights."

Need a divorce lawyer? Talk to one with 20 years' experience crafting effective relationship exit strategies.
MACLEAN FAMILY LAW GROUP 604.602.9000
www.bcfamilylaw.ca

PRACTICE-SPECIFIC

TRANSPORTATION LAW:
VEDDER PRICE

If you're in a well-worn practice area, attaining market leadership is a long shot. Even if you're among the smartest lawyers in that area, persuading a large segment of the potential audience of that is always difficult. That's the inherent challenge of having so darned many competitors. So you segment. By industry or practice or any of the many other ways we've mentioned.

Finance is another one of those "table of contents" practices. It's one all major firms list in their websites' drop-down menus. So why compete on their terms, when you could identify a subset you could own? Find or create a smaller target audience, and work to become the go-to practice in that area.

Vedder Price is a full-service firm that has a terrific corporate finance practice. But with offices in Chicago, New York, and London, they're competing against innumerable other firms, many much larger, that can also do those deals. It's hard to differentiate one finance practice from another. So, while their lawyers continue handling sophisticated finance deals, they earned global market leadership by targeting a few specialty areas, particularly in the transportation area.

Of course "transportation" is a general catch-all word. To Vedder Price, transportation means aircraft, railcars, and ships. Financing things that move around the country or around the world is different than financing, for example, medical equipment that won't be in a different time zone or continent the next day. So it requires special expertise.

To highlight Vedder Price's proficiency in this area, we created a niche marketing campaign for its high-powered specialty practice of handling major, sophisticated deals between investors and aircraft carriers, as well as between Big Money and maritime and rail corpo-

rations. When we worked with the firm, Vedder Price had 40 full-time transportation lawyers, making it one of the world's largest such practices.

Led by Dean Gerber, the friendly practice group chair, the group had a strong standing in the field. But, in a large international industry, Dean and his partners wanted to solidify their position and expand into new markets. So we helped them launch a series of bold new industry-specific advertisements.

Every industry has its own overused visual icons. As I mentioned earlier in the book, the legal profession can't seem to get enough of gavels, columns, dart boards, and puzzle pieces. In the transportation arena, the ads in the publications are packed, photo after photo, with planes, ships, trains, and other things that move stuff from one place to another. And frankly, after you've seen one picture of a cockpit or airplane sitting on a tarmac, you've essentially seen them all. We wanted to poke some gentle fun at this ho-hum marketing routine, while making Vedder Price stand proudly above its competitors.

To achieve this, we designed ads to counteract this worn-out, sad-sack advertising tradition, hinting at the industry clichés, while avoiding them entirely. Thus in the ad described above you see the jet contrail but not the airplane. In other ads you see the tracks but not the train, or the ocean, but not the ship. The clean design distinguishes the image and the message, making the reader stop and take notice. The ads do what they're supposed to do: Raise awareness.

Now let me show you that blue-sky ad:

And, check out this long, straight train track and the accompanying text; I think there's something very compelling about the image:

INDUSTRY FOCUS

AGRICULTURE LAW: NOLAND HAMERLY

Traditionally, law firms segment and organize their services—and their marketing—around administrative practice areas such as litigation, corporate, tax, employment, and so on. But that is changing. Firms recognize that many clients want attorneys who possess an in-depth understanding of a particular industry. Accounting firms have been organizing themselves by industry for decades.

An industry focus gives lawyers a broader grasp of a client's issues and problems. Further, because they're cross-functional, industry-based practices create more cross-selling opportunities. When a law firm can find a narrowly focused industry niche, it gives the attorneys a solid marketing advantage. Their advertisements, slogans, websites, and other marketing materials need to reflect this expertise. Note, we're talking here about narrow specialty industries, not the obvious ones like banking, construction, health care, insurance, and real estate. Those are just too big. We're thinking more in terms of "transportation of infectious materials," rather than "transportation law." Think "small molecule therapeutics" rather than "pharmaceutical law."

We became acquainted with Noland Hamerly Etienne & Hoss, PC, a full-service partnership in central California's beautiful Salinas Valley, when we assisted with its retreat and training program in 2006. The firm was looking to stave off aggressive new local competitors. Management asked us to help develop a strong marketing strategy—Nolan Hamerly's first campaign ever—that would increase its visibility and draw in more high-quality business from its home turf. And it needed to bring in new revenue immediately. Oh, and also, the budget was tight.

Often if you aim broadly at the business community as a full-service law firm, you encounter daunting and pricey challenges. That approach was just too general, too wide, too shallow. We decided to take another route, the deep-and-narrow path.

The fields of the rich valley farmland held the obvious answer. As I drove the hour to the firm from the San Jose airport, I saw mile after mile of lush land flourishing with crops like lettuce, spinach, tomatoes, artichokes, and broccoli. Noland Hamerly wanted to be known as one of California's leading business law firms. But this seemed too big, too grandiose.

Not that they weren't terrific lawyers. The problem was, there were simply so many outstanding firms across California to make them stand out. It would be an expensive effort, one that would ultimately be unlikely to succeed—there was just too much competition. With the firm's limited budget, to show results we would need to focus on a smaller target audience, one we could reach systematically and cost-effectively.

The answer seemed obvious—we would anoint Noland Hamerly as the region's go-to agriculture firm. No other firm had yet staked a claim on that territory, so it was—pardon the puns—fertile ground and ripe for the picking. They had a long history representing many sides of the agriculture industry (for example shippers, growers, vineyards, transportation, etc.); it had not occurred to them to attempt an industry-specific effort. They were simply bursting with potential.

We came up with a targeted ad campaign aimed at a specific audience: the fruit and produce industry that brings the crops of "America's Salad Bowl" to the market. Using a catchy and memorable alliteration, we named the multi-faceted agriculture-centered program "The Lettuce Lawyers," knowing that this simple tweak would act as a public relations hook and generate lots of free earned media. The tag line was the clever "Together We Grow."

We would use PR as a tool to build credibility with our legal and agriculture targets. The lawyers were comfortable playing along, so we had the opportunity to intentionally create marketing materials we knew would invariably lead to feature stories about the firm's unique

WE'RE SMART. WE'RE OLD. AND WE'RE THE BEST AT EVERYTHING.

agriculture industry practice. We weren't the first such practice; we simply wanted to be the best-known one, and positive publicity can help build awareness quickly.

We designed other materials to enhance both the credibility of the lawyers and the market-ability of the campaign. We created some little strategies to gain publicity, knowing, for example, that no other law firm had ever designed a unique logo specifically for an industry practice. Generating a collection of articles about that proved to be easy.

We had the agricultural logo stitched onto bib overalls and sent a few to clients, then told the media all about it. Logo'd bib overalls? From a law firm?! Another few feature stories were almost guaranteed.

We printed the lawyers' contact information on actual seed packets and handed them out as business cards at conferences, sending some to the media as well. More stories.

We saw that the US Postal Service had just started allowing private citizens to design their own stamps, and we re-printed one of the ads as official USPS stamps for mailings to agriculture clients. Still more feature stories.

Here's the larger point: Gaining publicity isn't hard if you find out what the media is looking for, and then hand-feed them what they want.

We were already redesigning the firm's primary website, so it was a relatively simple matter to create a complementary lettucelaw.com industry-specific microsite based upon the same design, illustrated by the advertising visuals.

WE'RE SMART. WE'RE OLD. AND WE'RE THE BEST AT EVERYTHING.

The farming-centered strategy was a tremendous success. The campaign increased the firm's visibility and grabbed the attention of the local agriculture community. Drawn by the buzz, new clients came to the firm, while delighted existing clients sent more business Nolan Hamerly's way. The Lettuce Law program received *Small Firm Business* magazine's 2006 Best Practices award for the nation's best marketing campaign.

It was, if you will, an abundant harvest.

INDUSTRY FOCUS

HEALTH CARE LAW: DRINKER BIDDLE

Ever since Grok, a prehistoric ancestor of ours, grunted out a story about mastodons and coconuts while scraping out accompanying imagery on the walls of his cave, we've been drawn in by storytelling. Simply put, everyone loves a good story. Find your stories. Tell your stories. Don't be afraid of the emotion or drama they contain. Instead, leverage it.

Consider Philadelphia-based Drinker Biddle's health care practice. A series of strategic mergers had quickly grown the firm from 200 to 700 lawyers and assembled one of the profession's finest health care industry practices.

Internal firm communications is a challenge in every law firm, a condition exacerbated here by the firm's rapid growth in numbers and offices. It's nearly impossible for busy professionals to stay in regular contact or keep a running inventory of every individual's personal experience. It's just the nature of a profession constructed around billable hours.

Over time, Drinker's health care practice had grown and diversified, adding many full-time health care lawyers and professionals, and others who had built leading practices in niche areas that touched health care who were not included in the main health care practice.

The firm recognized that they were not capitalizing on the tremendous health care talent scattered across the firm and its practices. They needed to somehow take stock of their internal resources, establish a more formal structure, increase the flow of communication that would lead to more cross-selling opportunities, and go to market boldly.

WE'RE SMART. WE'RE OLD. AND WE'RE THE BEST AT EVERYTHING.

We personally interviewed dozens of health care lawyers in various offices and practices, looking for their unique differentiator. It can be difficult to find one when a group is so diversified in practice and geography, particularly when cobbled together through rapid mergers. Firms often blend practices without considering personality or fit. In those cases, you can find skilled professionals, but not a culture that binds them. Our interviews are designed in part to help us identify whether such a common style exists.

We discovered that the health care practice had a significant presence in the not-for-profit sector. The lawyers closely identified with their clients' mission of providing quality health care to the public; they proudly talked about their clients' good work. In one of my very first one-on-one interviews, a senior associate teared-up when discussing the people who would be helped when she was finally able to figure out how to help a client get regulatory approval for a life-changing new product. Another proudly told me the story of how her work for a client enabled children with cancer in far-flung rural communities to receive their ongoing chemo treatments at home, rather than needing to drive two hours each way to the medical facility.

Their palpable investment in their clients' success gave me an idea for a powerful marketing message. But first I wanted to make sure I felt that same commitment from the other group members. Twenty-five interviews later, I found a remarkable level of consistency. Across the nation, the Drinker Biddle lawyers were all-in. We had a theme.

We looked one step farther than usual—on benefits, not features. Rather than discussing the firm's fine legal work, in, for example, helping bring useful products to market, we focused farther downstream, on the end users of the firm's services, that is, the real people who would be benefiting from the products and innovations their lawyers helped effectuate. Like the grateful kids with cancer who could finally receive their care at home.

In the course of the interviews, we also identified another 40 Drinker lawyers with sufficient health care expertise to be added to the practice group, along with five other related specialty areas. We created a message and marketing campaign with a robust website to tell the clients' powerful stories.

Using poignant imagery, the case study-based platform describes the great work done in each of Drinker's 14 health care-related practice areas, and shows how proud the lawyers are to contribute to their clients achieving their goals. The lawyers were one more link in the chain of providing quality health care to those who need it.

We felt this tag line captures the spirit of the service the health care attorneys provide: "Helping health care clients do good."

The full-service firm had recently upgraded its main website, offering 250+ distinct practice areas. Like all big-firm websites, its organization was firmly in place and did not offer much room for flexibility. Our marketing message and materials were so radically different from the firm's conservative approach that we couldn't effectively squeeze it into the firm's formal structure.

Now at the time, it was unusual for a law firm to relinquish control of its primary website and allow a practice group to break away, so to speak, and do its own site. But Rob McCann, one of the leaders of the flourishing health care group and a genuine strategic thinker, convinced the firm's management to let him oversee a team to develop an industry-specific website.

One of the most-important aspects of all of this was how it permitted the firm's internal team to pull everyone together. We launched this major initiative at a two-day retreat, where the lawyers all told their wonderful client stories and started the heartfelt dialog that led to the health care team working together more closely and cross-selling more services to valued clients nationwide.

Below is an example of the new health care-specific microsite:

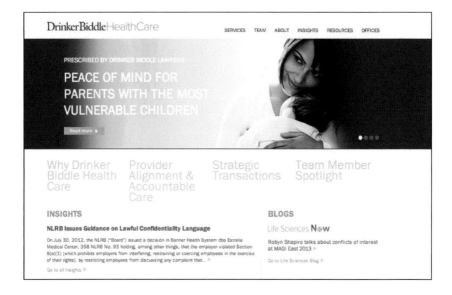

We were proud of our work and the Drinker team was very enthusiastic about the new campaign.

Here are two more:

NICHE MARKETING

BORKAN & SCAHILL
FB RICE & CO.

If your law firm has a specific niche practice needing publicity, you have to create a bit of a buzz. Or, perhaps, a big electric-charged jolt.

What would you do to show your firm is deadly serious about defending police officers in civil rights cases?

The website of Chicago's Borkan & Scahill describes Steve Borkan as "a seasoned trial lawyer." That's putting it mildly. Steve is a charismatic and gregarious attorney, a former actor and nationally ranked trampolinist, and a brilliant strategist. He defends insurance companies, often in large, politically sensitive cases. He also advocates for municipalities and public agencies such as police departments.

Steve maintains a specialty representing police officers in civil rights cases that often involve charges of police misconduct. Today, these are often brought as "excessive force" cases. Wanting firsthand insight into how to more effectively fight for these cop clients, and agreeing that it would also be a powerful marketing maneuver, Steve took action. Because many of his cases involve the increasingly common allegation of inappropriate electroshock weapon use, he persuaded police instructors to let him join an official training class on these stunning tools.

At the end, he eagerly volunteered to be tased, to feel the plaintiffs' experience. We suggested that this act would be advantageous for marketing purposes—but only if he could videotape it on his phone. Steve is fearless, but he is not stupid.

It went about as you might expect. … He was brought to his knees, screaming. Now there's a guy committed to serving his clients.

But it was worth it. Steve gained keen insight for cross-examinations and serious street cred for his firm. And the video ensured that we could easily arrange feature stories in national publications, covering him as one of the industry's leading experts in this niche. A video of a lawyer getting tased? The media was climbing over each other to write the story. See the video here from the American Bar Association's *ABA Journal* article: *https://goo.gl/DbYlWV*

It's not always necessary, however, to get tased, shocked, and stunned in the interest of good marketing for a niche. There's always the "use a catchy marketing campaign" option. It's effective, and frankly far less painful than taking tens of thousands of volts of electricity.

FB Rice & Co. is an Australian intellectual property firm that specializes in brand protection for that nation's wine industry. It was a 40-lawyer firm that had developed market leadership by combining three things:

1. A practice area (intellectual property), with

2. An industry (wine), and

3. A geography (Australia).

WE'RE SMART. WE'RE OLD. AND WE'RE THE BEST AT EVERYTHING.

This seems quite narrow, but they knew that Australia had a large and vibrant wine industry that was facing some serious intellectual property challenges, especially relating to brand protection. Wine consumers were becoming more brand-conscious, and the vintners were increasingly using creative names and labels to encourage purchasing. In many cases, the brands were becoming as, if not more, important, than the wine itself. It was vital that the wine companies protect their valuable trademarks.

We developed an advertising and direct mail campaign and an industry-specific micro-website that focused on their unique industry expertise and understanding of this important issue. Ad headlines included:

> *The label is as important as your wine.*

> *If you don't protect the label, the wine can go bad.*

> *Protecting your label is as crucial as protecting what's inside.*

These materials helped the firm strengthen its hold on its large-but-focused target market.

And, as they say Down Under, that campaign was bonzer.

LITIGATION STRENGTHS

HOWARD LAW GROUP
RUMBERGER KIRK & CALDWELL
SEGAL MCCAMBRIDGE
FIGLIULO+SILVERMAN
SEBALY SHILLITO

When I look around the legal profession and analyze law firm marketing, I'm always surprised to see law firms run from their strengths. It's almost like they're intentionally hiding their assets, which of course harms their brand. I could offer several examples, but, in the spirit of civility, I'll decline. You can probably think of some on your own, those exceptional firms that have somehow succeeded in looking common.

By the way, the firms don't do it on purpose; it's just that they sometimes can't properly identify what they're good at, or somehow think their skills aren't worth highlighting. When our team goes inside a law firm we do everything we can to uncover the lawyers' strengths and feature them—often focusing on the most powerful asset—in the marketing campaign we design for the firm.

For example, earlier in the book I mentioned the small but super-successful trial boutique in Grand Rapids, the Howard Law Group. Bill Howard, his partner and wife Jean and their team know how to win … and win … and win. Their courtroom won-loss record is off the charts. So our marketing efforts screamed: "We win!"

•••

Or consider Florida-based Rumberger, Kirk & Caldwell. As human beings they're a friendly and collegial bunch of people. But as litigators at trial, they're hard-nosed combatants who push, and push back, firmly. Consequently, we created this tag line: "Your Lawyer Should be Tough."

Florida's ethics rules prohibit comparative claims, so we couldn't actually say that *they* were tough, we just suggested that your lawyer *should* be tough, and let the reader infer from the headline that the Rumberger lawyers probably fit the bill. And the cleverly exaggerated visuals, implying that they eat nails for breakfast, shave with hunting knives, and drink hot sauce, among other tough activities, grabbed viewers' attention. (The favorite example of overstatement was the roll of toilet paper made out of sandpaper, but we think classy law firms should avoid potty humor, so we never ran it.)

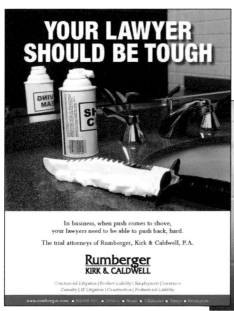

When it came to helping another national insurance-litigation firm, Segal McCambridge Singer & Mahoney, we identified their unique philosophy and went with it. A mid-sized firm of renowned class-action lawyers, Segal McCambridge defends significant national cases, like asbestos and latex gloves. This litigation almost always involves complex issues of facts, law, science, and biology, spread among hundreds or thousands of cases across dozens of jurisdictions.

To come out on top for their clients, they have to distill each case's complexities into concepts and language the average juror can understand; they simplify the layers of medical, legal, and scientific facts into compelling stories so the juries "get it." The campaign we created pokes gentle fun at certain jurors, showing the difficulty the SMSM lawyers face. It was a multifaceted marketing initiative that included three central figures, which we picked up in ads, a brochure, logo, and website. The simple tag line encapsulates their differentiation in five words: "We make the complex simple."

Here are the two of the brand visuals:

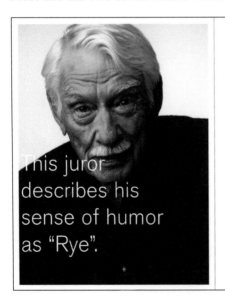

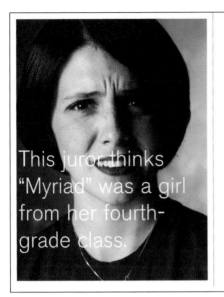

This juror thinks "Myriad" was a girl from her fourth-grade class.

And it's our job to help her understand the epidemiological distinctions between mild tricuspid valvular regurgitation, endothelialized foreign matter, and bacterial endocarditis.

So much law firm marketing materials are dense, dull, and unread, and the marketing toward insurance companies is even worse. Lawyers view insurance companies as conservative, so the marketing aimed at them is pretty stiff. We view things differently. Insurance companies are not giant cement and steel monoliths, they're *people*, and people don't like to be bored. They're not going to volunteer to read uninspiring marketing materials.

So Segal McCambridge took a calculated risk by approving something lighter. The result? The firm's insurance clients were actually calling the firm to request *more* copies of the brochure. We learned that they were getting passed all across the insurance companies, and clients and prospects were taping the humorous visuals to their cubicle walls.

Shortly after the partners rolled out this campaign, they started seeing significantly more work walk in the door, underscoring this credo: Strengths sell.

•••

Of course, not every litigation firm needs to sell strength or toughness; there are many ways to win a case.

Working with Figliulo & Silverman, we learned that that firm doesn't seek to overpower competitors, but rather to outsmart them. As Jim Figliulo describes it, he looks for "the one essential truth" that exists in every case, the one fact or issue he can hang his hat on, then uses that to lever a victory with the judge or jury. This strategy has proven wildly successful for him in major cases against much larger firms. As we described it on the website home page:

> "It may be hidden by complications, difficulties, or seemingly insurmountable obstacles, but there is always a truthful position that would allow you to succeed. We must find that truth, have the strength and wisdom to advocate it, and thereby craft a just and genuine victory."

With this point in mind, we built a brand supported by two architectural elements, an arch and a keystone, that acted analogously.

THE RIGHT IDEA CONNECTS ALL THE PIECES.

The Keystone at the peak of a masonry arch locks the stones into position, strengthening the entire structure. Without it, everything collapses. It's the essential element, the single idea that connects the disparate pieces and joins them powerfully together. The simplest solution distilled to its very essence will stand the test of time. At Figliulo & Silverman, we are builders. We are story-tellers. We are trial lawyers.

F+S Figliulo & Silverman, P.C.
WHERE THE FIGHTING SPIRIT LIVES.

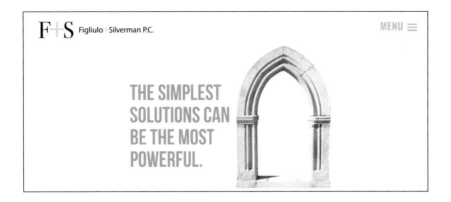

A single keystone locks the stones in an arch into position and strengthens the entire structure. As we phrased it on the home page (fslegal.com):

> "While the arch is one of the simplest architectural ideas, it enabled ancient architects to build soaring cathedrals and the monumental Coliseum. The same can be said of litigation, where the simplest idea can often be the most powerful. But simple doesn't mean easy. Simple requires thinking more strategically, working more efficiently, and accomplishing client goals more effectively. And at Figliulo & Silverman, simple succeeds."

•••

Litigation firms can also highlight specific differentiation traits. One of Ohio's finest litigation practices, Dayton-based Sebaly Shillito + Dyer was a market leader in handling business litigation cases on contingency. During the recession, litigation filings plummeted because plaintiffs couldn't afford the legal fees, so even plaintiffs with winning cases struggled to find commercial lawyers willing to take their cases.

SS&D's Litigation Department chair Jim Dyer knew how to evaluate those complex cases. He knew that companies were feeling frustrated that the wrongdoer would get away with the misconduct. Jim offered a way for them to cost-effectively protect their rights, which made the clients heroes within their companies. This idea formed the basis of our client-oriented advertising campaign.

Who doesn't love a super hero?

Let Sebaly Shillito + Dyer lawyers help make you a hero. **We share the risks and rewards of lawsuits by taking many business cases on a contingency.** We'll help you or your clients fight tough adversaries without blowing the budget. **Learn more at www.ssdlaw.com/contingency or call Toby Henderson at 937.222.2500.**

ss+d

SEBALY SHILLITO + DYER
A LEGAL PROFESSIONAL ASSOCIATION
WE'VE GOT YOUR BACK
Dayton + West Chester

LET SEBALY SHILLITO + DYER BUSINESS LAWYERS HELP MAKE YOU A HERO.
We share the risks and rewards of lawsuits by taking many business cases on a contingency. We'll help fight tough adversaries without blowing the budget.

PERSONALITY

THE COLLINS LAW FIRM

To outsiders, law firms tend to look alike. But they're often microcosms of the founders or leaders' personalities or core values. As we've shown, some firms are tougher, more creative, or more service oriented. Whatever you are has helped make you successful. There's a target audience for that. If you have a particular trait that your clients value, be proud of it. Tell more people your story—showcasing a colorful or distinct personality can be an excellent marketing strategy.

Take The Collins Law Firm. Founded as a spin-off from a large Chicago firm, the lawyers at this scrappy litigation boutique pride themselves on their take-no-prisoners approach. A small firm operating out of a western suburb of Chicago, they were frequently getting mistaken as a general-practice firm that handles small local consumer matters, like house closings, wills, and traffic tickets.

The reality couldn't be any more different. The Collins Law Firm handles large, sophisticated, complex litigation cases, often going up against some of the nation's largest litigation firms and practices. They just liked doing it from the suburbs.

The firm is led by founding partner Shawn Collins, a thoughtful, pull-no-punches litigator. Shawn is aggressive in life, litigation, and marketing, a nice guy who fights fiercely for his clients. In our intake interviews, Shawn detailed his historic affinity for representing the smaller party who's up against larger corporations or law firms. He finds it more rewarding to protect the little guy, the underdog, against whoever is trying to bully them.

During the interview, he realized that he'd always been like this—in middle school he would stand up for the little kid against the schoolyard bully. Shawn was now doing this with a law degree. That was who he was. That was how he approached his cases. That became the firm he'd formed.

That needed to be his message, because people and professionals can relate to being bullied.

So we developed a range of visuals that told that story, a law firm that stands up to corporate bullies. And Shawn loved the ads; they really did convey his approach. We were all happy with it. But our team had developed one more ad, consisting of a single powerful visual. We loved the idea but were concerned might be a touch too strong. Near the end of the meeting, we showed it to Shawn, who laughed out loud, long and hard. He said, "That's *me!* That's how I practice law!"

Then he called in his entire team and showed them the ad. They started laughing so hard they could barely choke out their approval, "Oh my God, that's *you!* That's *us!*"

They insisted that they use that ad instead. A simple wingtip shoe. The three-word headline showed an arrow pointing to the tip of the shoe: "Apply to butt." In 1999, this type of message was considered shocking.

We also learned that Shawn disagreed with the "civility" movement that was gaining momentum at the time. He believed that the emphasis on politeness and lawyers being nice to each other in litigation is not necessarily in the clients' best interests. "Clients don't want me to be nice to my opponents; they want me to win. They hate the stress of being in litigation. They don't want me to agree to requested continuances to be nice—they want this case to be over as quickly as possible, so I'm going to hold their feet to the fire every chance I get."

Other litigators agreed with Shawn's sentiment, but none had the courage to say so publicly. Shawn didn't mind being a lightning rod. When you have a client willing to be strategically controversial, public relations can be a powerful marketing weapon. Shawn would stand up for his convictions, which would make it easy for us to generate publicity and op-ed articles for him.

These pieces created additional publicity and an appearance at a bar association Civility Conference, where he faced off against some the bar's most outspoken civility supporters. Although controversial in legal circles and genteel Inns of Court meetings, his "anti-civility" stance positioned him firmly on the side of the clients.

The text summarizes their story: "In a business fight, you have to put your foot down. When this happens you just might need a bare-knuckled trial lawyer to make the bully go pick on someone his own size. The Collins Law Firm has that kind of lawyer. We're tough-minded and aggressive. We demand results ... and send the bullies back home. Think we can help you? Contact ..."

Message received.

The advertising and marketing program helped put Collins on the Chicago map. It also created an entirely new image for the firm, both internally and externally. In short order, the firm obtained several significant new clients who cold-called the firm in direct response to the ad. The attorneys attracted significant free publicity as national publications featured the campaign as an example of unique marketing. In fact, one magazine slashed its advertising rate because they were so interested in running the Collins Law Firm advertisement in their publication.

As a bonus, it became the central focus of the firm's recruiting, making a fine barometer to evaluate new lawyers' compatibility with the firm. Simply put, candidates who were uncomfortable with the message weren't a good long-term fit at the firm and not hired. But lawyers who saw the "Apply to Butt" ad, laughed, and exclaimed, "That's ME!" thereby passed the final test.

Ain't that a kick in the pants?

NAME-BASED MARKETING

GOOD NAMES:
SMART & BIGGAR
BEST, BEST & KRIEGER

What's in a name? Well, the short answer is … *a hell of a lot.*

A great name makes marketing easier. Corporations that pick an easy, memorable name lending itself to a visual symbol—Shell Oil, Target Stores, Apple Computers—have a leg up on their competitors. Iconic symbols translate into any language, and marketing flows seamlessly from the image the name conjures up.

Law firms, however, are stuck, for better or worse, with the names of their founders and grand poohbah partners. In many cases, firms must contend with a hard-to-spell, difficult-to-pronounce mouthful. Take, for example, the firm Ungaretti & Harris, where I used to be the marketing partner. Rich Ungaretti is a great guy and terrific lawyer, but his surname made marketing the firm a bit more complicated. His name was just a challenge we accepted and conquered.

Some partnerships, however, are gifted with fabulous roll-off-the-tongue names—names that stick in people's minds and instantly conjure strong images. The problem is, not all of these firms feel comfortable capitalizing on their good fortune. Some don't want to hit people over the head, or don't want to appear to be boorish, or just think it's all too obvious.

Generally, these firms are making a mistake by not grabbing their golden opportunity. Not only that, they take the chance that they look foolish and vacuous for failing to make the most of a memorable, evocative name.

Best, Best & Krieger is an example of a firm that had never leveraged its name in its marketing because of the hubris concern. The lawyers liked their existing "BB&K" initials logo, so we developed a "Best"-

WE'RE SMART. WE'RE OLD. AND WE'RE THE BEST AT EVERYTHING.

oriented campaign that kept the connection to the initials and also focused on their industry leadership and diversity initiatives. And, of course, we took advantage of the superlative-laden name, creating slogans such as:

- Your Best Case Scenario
- We Always Make the Best of Bad Situations
- Honesty is the Best Policy. So Are Results.

We always make the Best of bad situations.

Since the early 1910's, Best Best & Krieger has been serving California's fastest growing communities with legal advice in virtually all practice areas, including noteworthy work in school and municipal law, real estate, zoning and labor. Our more than 185 attorneys in eight strategically located offices offer unique experience in handling complex, multi-disciplinary issues and providing solutions of common interest to leaders of both business and government. If you want to work with the Best, give us a call or visit us online at bbklaw.com.

BBK | BEST BEST & KRIEGER
Attorneys at Law

Experience Experience & Results.

If your firm name contains a positive word—a noun, verb, or adjective that can be used to hook your audience and connect to your larger strategy or message—you most likely want to take it and run with it. But here's a caveat: Don't run too far or too fast. Doing name-based marketing does require finesse, and it isn't hard to go overboard.

Not every single interesting name can or should be used; it's just one more idea to be explored while developing a marketing or branding campaign or website.

You want creativity, but not a pun or a joke that induces groans or eye rolls. You don't want to be the firm elbowing people sharply in the ribs: *"Get it!? Huh? Get it???"*

•••

Smart & Biggar, which bills itself as "Canada's largest IP firm," has an almost ridiculously memorable and advantageous name. They are *literally* smart and bigger. (You can't make this stuff up.) My opinion is that when the play on your name, either positive *or* negative, is *so* obvious, it's incumbent on you to at least acknowledge that you're in on the joke. Failing to at least mention it in passing suggests that you're either too insecure to use it, or too dim to notice, neither of which are especially positive traits in a law firm.

Obviously, you must be careful to not seem too self-aggrandizing. It's okay to brag about yourself a bit—but do it with a wink, to let people know you're not taking yourself too seriously and are in on the joke. Smart & Biggar isn't a client, but they're a terrific firm. I'd like to see them use something like this, perhaps:

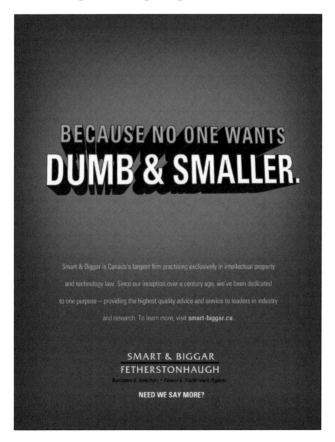

NAME-BASED MARKETING

CHALLENGING NAMES:
LOW, BALL & LYNCH
STEVENS VIRGIN

Not every law firm is fortuitously named. Law firm names aren't selected strategically for memorability, ease of speaking or spelling, or online searches. Traditionally, the prioritization of the names reflected the relative size of the founders' books of business.

As a result, a few firms are blessed with golden monikers like Best, Best & Krieger, or Smart & Biggar. Most are neutral and evoke no particular image or impression. And then there are the names that are dreadful, non-fiction versions of Dewey, Cheatum & Howe.

Take, for example, San Francisco insurance litigation firm Low, Ball & Lynch. Think we made that name up? Think again. It's real. And it's, shall we say, problematic.

How would a firm get saddled with a name like that? you might ask. The answer here is, organically. In this case, the founder, Mr. Low, hired a partner, Mr. Ball. Then Mr. Lynch came aboard. As names were added dutifully and sequentially, a memorably terrible law firm name was created. The firm didn't have a great sense of humor regarding the name; they simply chose to ignore the snickering "lowball" jokes, actually convincing themselves that lowball had a positive connotation to their insurance defense clients. "Our clients like that we make lowball offers."

How do you solve a problem like "Low Ball?" First, you take ownership. You project confidence. Then you perform marketing jiu jitsu and flip the negative into a positive.

If you have a difficult, negative, challenging, or downright embarrassing name, yes, you can use it to your advantage. (Consider "With a name like Smucker's, it has to be good." ®) A bad name is inherently memorable; the trick is figuring out how to use it effectively, with a delicate touch.

Or you can at least soften the edges and let people know you're in on the joke. With Low Ball, we confronted the obvious negative connotations of "lowball" and took advantage of the humor, juxtaposing "Low Ball" with "High Standards."

This unique name offered the opportunity to go much bolder and funnier (our creative team had some ideas they were dying to deploy), but they would not have been in keeping with the firm's conservative and understated personality. ...Perhaps we'll give Payne & Fears a call.

•••

"Virgin" is another word that's not exactly ideal to appear in a law firm name. But in the case of Vancouver's StevensVirgin, we were able to take a weak word, a synonym for "inexperienced" and "naïve," and use it to make the firm stick in people's minds.

Name partner Mark Virgin, one of Vancouver's top litigators, hired us to develop a marketing campaign and website to build the firm's local brand for referrals, particularly in the legal community. There was a looming Canadian Bar Association national conference in Vancouver where the firm would have a booth. As a small litigation boutique, they wanted to use this CBA event to build name recognition and seek referrals from across Canada.

As we've seen, one has a choice in marketing. You can either pretend you don't notice an obvious obstacle or undesirable element, or you can embrace it, own it, and take advantage of it. Mr. Virgin, a talented, practical, and, yes, handsome attorney, realized that it was time he leveraged his name and harnessed its positive powers. (We felt particularly good about that, imagining what his middle-school years must have been like.)

So, we created a campaign that cemented the firm's unique name in the Canadian legal community's mind. By embracing its "virginity," so to speak, the firm reinforced both its expertise and culture. See for yourself:

Want a lawyer with experience?

Go with a VIRGIN.

stevens**VIRGIN**

LITIGATION COUNSEL / *law corporations*

www.stevensvirgin.com

The Hire a Virgin campaign made the firm the hit of the conference. The Virgin initiative created a big buzz there, which significantly boosted its visibility and standing within the national legal community. People scooped up Virgin-related swag, as well; the "Go with a Virgin" coffee mugs were the hottest giveaway and supplies soon ran short. So they collected hundreds of business cards and shipped follow-up mugs across Canada after the conference.

The firm also markets to a lay-consumer audience. We knew that this Virgin theme might not play quite as well with average folks who'd been injured in an accident, so we later toned it down on the website to ensure the firm's message was received well by the broader community.

And that's how we conquered Virgin marketing territory.

NAME-BASED MARKETING

USEFUL NAMES:
FLASTER/GREENBERG
GLENN FELDMANN

We've taken a look at marketing approaches to firms with both un-usually good and unusually bad names. Most partnerships have names that are neutral, neither evoking a cringe nor a positive reaction. Expanded name recognition, however, is a key goal of marketing, no matter what the name. And there is often a way to make a name even more memorable.

Flaster/Greenberg is an entrepreneurial regional firm in the New York, New Jersey, and Eastern Pennsylvania area, competing against similarly sized and large well-known contenders.

The firm contacted Fishman Marketing seeking help updating the look and feel of their new website. A web-development company had created a technologically sound platform that failed to brand or differentiate the firm. Fancy bells and whistles—like animated graphics on the home page—did little to tell the firm's story or give it a distinctive identity.

The firm's new marketing director, Anne Matlack, saw an opportunity to upgrade and create a new look and feel for the site, capitalizing on the firm's energetic environment. We saw how we could use the firm's strong and memorable first name "Flaster" as a play on "Faster," while leveraging the unique horizontal green stripes on their logo.

Through in-person interviews with the firm's lawyers and professionals, we identified the message to potential clients (often owners and senior executives of closely held entrepreneurial middle-market businesses): Flaster has practical, efficient, hard-working, no-BS, get-the-job-done lawyers. They find the fastest, best, most-efficient way to get from A to Z. Clients work directly with the partners they hire. The firm is business-oriented and well run by a smart, efficient management team.

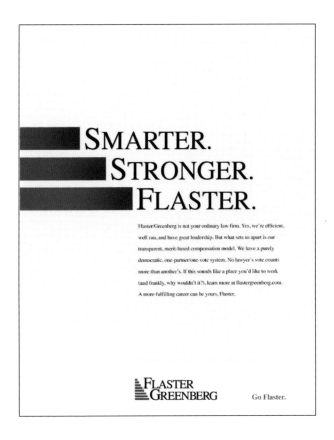

The message to potential lateral hires: Flaster is a firm for lawyers who are entrepreneurial, have their own book of business, and love to practice law. The fixed and fair Flaster compensation formula takes the politically messy crap out of the practice of law, so partners can act like partners.

We launched a visual campaign as the foundation to update the website. We also created ads to target local lawyers for lateral hiring. A separate ad campaign built the firm's brand for client-development purposes.

"Go Flaster" helps initiate the conversation.

•••

The Roanoke, VA firm of Glenn, Feldmann, Darby & Goodlatte is a high-quality small firm that's home to some of that region's leading lawyers. In a competitive market, the firm continued to excel, although its marketing remained traditional and unremarkable. The partnership decided to hire us to overhaul its promotional approach.

The firm, commonly known as "Glenn Feldmann," has an unusual "double n" name. The challenge was that it sounds like the name of a person, not a law firm. The opportunity came in the unique way we could leverage the moniker for marketing purposes, to help tell its creative story.

Although the name is strong and easy to spell and remember, its logo had been focused on its initials rather than the words.

original logo

We redesigned the logo to reinforce the name and its memorable double n's and launched a new marketing campaign with a series of print ads that emphasized the spelling.

The firm's name also provided the hook we needed to showcase the firm's well-known individual lawyers, who appeared in ads with the tagline "I am Glenn Feldmann. And there are a lot more just like us."

BEING DIFFERENT

BALCH & BINGHAM

If there's one theme you take away from this book, let it be this:

Trash tired clichés.

Smash the same old, same old.

Reject regular.

Deviate from dull.

It pays to be different, creative, eye-catching, memorable, bold. And getting noticed doesn't have to be costly.

When several Balch & Bingham lawyers were selected as "Top Lawyers" for a legal publication, the Birmingham, AL firm wanted to buy an ad to support their firm's strong showing. Now, I generally dislike these types of ads and vanity publications; there's no convincing evidence that clients ever hire their lawyers based upon ads in these advertorial directories.

But, once the magazine's salespeople had persuaded the firm's lawyers to buy an ad, Balch & Bingham's savvy Client Services Director Nora Chandler didn't want the typical boilerplate, let's-pat-ourselves-on-the-back boring ad that other firms were certain to produce.

You've seen these things. They feature a group of buttoned-up lawyers looking stiff and uncomfortable, grinning awkwardly in a carefully composed shot. You can just imagine the photographer giving instructions. "Okay, Dave, please straighten your tie a bit. Ann, could you rotate your head a tad to the right? Now, on the count of 'three,' look *natural.*" These Studiously Serious Shots are usually accompanied by a generic three-word alliterative description like: "Experienced. Excellent. Expertise." or "Smart. Skilled. Savvy."

Ho hum. No readers pay attention to these pricey ads except perhaps for the photographed lawyers themselves. And their moms.

Nora called us asking for something completely different. She wanted to create an ad that would make a splash, stand out, and showcase the firm's friendly personality. It also had to include information about the attorneys who'd been honored by the publication.

"Let's stand out" is our creative teams' favorite mission, and we showed her a range of options guaranteed to succeed. Nora selected the image of a bulldog with a cigar. Naturally.

The inexpensive royalty-free photo did the job. It caught people's attention and made them smile. It conveyed a sense of confidence and humor rather than self-importance. Readers couldn't help but stop and read the firm name and the headline: "What? You'd rather see another picture of a bunch of lawyers in suits?"

And what did you see when you turned the page? You guessed it ... ad after forgettable ad of "grinning lawyers in suits." Zzzzzzzz.

The Balch ad stood out boldly, confidently, and memorably—and it immediately created enormous local buzz, winning some national marketing awards as well.

Our ad cost exactly the same as the others in the publication. But anyone skimming through would see 100+ identical immediately forgettable groups of lawyers. And then they'd see ours. And they'd only remember ours.

The right type of creativity makes every dollar you spend work harder for you. And if you're not going to expect your marketing to work, why bother doing it at all?

GEOGRAPHY

CARLTON FIELDS, ATLANTA
LACAZ MARTINS, RIO DE JANEIRO

When a firm stakes out new territory by moving into a different geographic region, an aggressive marketing push is just what's needed to get the branch off the ground.

Carlton Fields was an eight-office, full-service firm, and one of the oldest in the Sunshine State. For years it was firmly established as "The Florida Firm." Its decision to open an Atlanta office, its first outside of its home state, presented a recruiting challenge.

The firm signed a lease for substantial office space and set its sights on quickly filling the new facilities with high-level partners from Atlanta's best firms. But that plan hit a roadblock. Even though Carlton Fields was a top-notch Florida firm, few people in the Atlanta legal profession were familiar with its name. And leading lawyers don't return the calls of headhunters who are seeking candidates for a firm they've never heard of.

Problematically, several prominent national and regional firms were also opening Atlanta offices at that time, increasing the competition for lateral recruiting. Most of those firms had similar name-recognition problems, and few of these newcomers were truly fighting to get noticed.

Our research resulted in a campaign that targeted the local bar to boost Carlton Fields' lateral-hiring prospects. We saw a great opportunity to leverage its Florida dominance in order to gain credibility and highlight the recent studies that gave the firm high marks for friendliness and quality-of-life. Additionally, because the Atlanta market was awash in law firm ads, the materials needed to jump out at the viewer.

We came up with vibrant, humorous, bright-orange ads that played off features associated with Florida (sunburns, beaches, palm trees, and alligators) and Georgia (peaches and the city's skyline). The tagline read: "Carlton Fields. Florida's Law Firm, now in Atlanta."

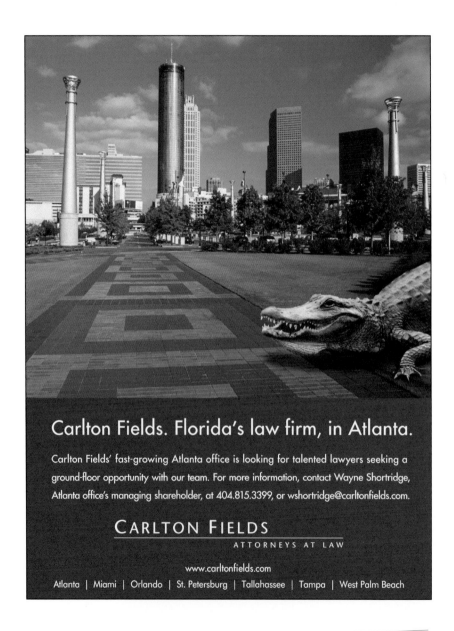

WE'RE SMART. WE'RE OLD. AND WE'RE THE BEST AT EVERYTHING.

Fortunately, a well-read local legal publication, the *Fulton County Daily Report*, was a good fit as our initial advertising platform. Instead of rolling out the campaign over a long period of time, we instead chose to hit Atlanta over the head with a "shock and awe" strategy that inundated the city's legal market in just a few weeks. That way any other recent-arrival firm that realized it should also be making a marketing splash wouldn't be able to play catch up—even if it scrambled.

The campaign attained massive visibility in the Atlanta legal community—and the ads were not only initially noticed, they stuck in people's heads. Previously a no-name firm in Atlanta, within a month Carlton Fields achieved over 90 percent market penetration with local lawyers. Not only did most of the Atlanta lawyers we surveyed comment approvingly on the content, they remembered the message—the name of the firm, its Florida roots, and that it was seeking laterals. Name recognition soared among local lawyers, and in-person recruiting success tripled. Carlton Fields was able to quickly hire the quality lawyers they'd been searching for.

And what did this entire campaign cost Carlton Fields? *Less than half of one headhunter fee.* Smart recruiters understand that marketing can be their best friend.

What's the point? Before invading new territory we softened the beachhead by shoring up our foothold—name recognition—before we marched on Atlanta, so to speak. And you can use this tactic to your advantage, too. That is, use marketing and branding to build your name recognition and visibility with your target audience before you start your recruiting efforts, and you'll increase your chance of swift success. Presume the new market has never heard of you (that's generally a pretty safe bet), and work to build interest and excitement in your firm before setting loose the recruiters. Effective geography-based marketing can attract more and better candidates, making the recruiters' job much easier and more productive, or obviate the need for them entirely.

Wouldn't it be nice if the top lateral candidates were calling *you* for a change?

One more recommendation regarding geography—when working in foreign markets it's very important to ensure you understand the culture and the ethics rules. Legal marketing in Asia or South America is conservative, so a humorous or aggressive style that would be successful in the United States could be considered inappropriate or unethical. Similarly, an ad that would work in New York City could be considered too much for a smaller rural US community. If you're ever unsure, I'd recommend running the ad by some members of your target audience, just to ensure you're on safe ground.

•••

Here, for example, is an ad we designed for a Brazilian law firm, using Rio de Janeiro's famous Christ the Redeemer statue. It's a funny, eye-catching ad, but one we elected not to run in the United States, where religion can be a hot-button issue. Our testing indicated that some members of our target audience could be offended. We decided that it wasn't worth the risk to run it, because we had other good options that, while not quite as clever, posed zero risk.

TESTIMONIALS

GARVEY SCHUBERT BARER
FORDE LAW

Sometimes there's nothing like a good old-fashioned testimonial to sell your firm to the world.

Getting the thumbs-up from a respected person, company, or institution can strongly support your own positive assertions about your firm. Testimonials serve as a sort of proof that your lawyers really are skilled or experienced or tough or caring—or whatever angle you're emphasizing.

Effective testimonials can build trust, demonstrate success, and strengthen your credibility. There is something about another objective party singing your praises that makes potential clients feel much more confident about giving your firm a try. (They help sell books, too. That's why, like so many other authors, I solicited testimonials for this book. Sometimes all you have to do is ask and you shall receive.)

Seattle's Garvey Schubert Barer is an international but relatively small firm that competes with the largest firms in the Pacific Northwest. After conducting the intake interviews with then-CMO Melissa Hoff, we realized that the firm represented many more large and sophisticated clients than might be expected from a firm its size.

We decided a testimonial-based campaign would be just the thing to validate GSB's skills. Having existing "customers" give their endorsements would be far more persuasive than simply pointing out that the firm represents prominent companies, which is a claim that sounds like the claim of every other firm—savvy prospects read that language with skepticism. Specifically naming clients (*always* with client permission) is a step better, but there's always a question about how much work you actually did for them.

But if a client values you enough to allow you to use them in something as public as advertising or a website banner, you must have a true trusting relationship. And that speaks volumes.

Of course, many of your best clients will have official corporate policies forbidding this type of use. Others might want to help, but will decline anyway, worried about what their other law firms will say—and what if their accountants and management consultants want to use them too? ... What's more, few clients want to be used as a litigation or employment law success story ("Our firm successfully beat down another sexual harassment case for XYZ Company, our third victory in a row for the CEO!"). And once they run it up the corporate flagpole, you'll likely need to placate the company's own marketing department, who will inevitably want to edit your brilliant marketing verbiage into something less elegant or effective. It ain't easy, but under the right circumstances, it's still worth the aggravation.

Garvey Schubert Barer forged ahead with the testimonial campaign. Here's what the ads looked like and how a few of them read:

OUR RELATIONSHIP WITH CHATEAU STE. MICHELLE
KEEPS GETTING BETTER WITH AGE

We're proud to continue assisting Chateau Ste. Michelle since their early beginnings.
Here's to them and a strong future together.

GSB.LAW NEW YORK, NEW YORK PORTLAND, OREGON SEATTLE, WASHINGTON WASHINGTON, DC

GARVEY
SCHUBERT
BARER

Using strong photos of famous and prominent clients, we highlight-
ed the firm's remarkable representations and leveraged its existing
strong orange-colored brand. Clients included Venus and Serena
Williams ("Whatever court they enter, we'll help them win.") and
InFocus LCD projectors ("We've helped InFocus see their vision.").

After a successful run, we were asked to refresh the campaign three
years later by the firm's new CMO with a campaign we built off the
firm's well-known triangular orange shape in its logo.

GARVEY HELPS
PARR LUMBER
BUILD THE
FUTURE.

Garvey Schubert Barer lawyers. We've
built a strong partnering relationship
over the last 75 years, helping them grow
from a one-store, family business into a
regional building-supply powerhouse.
That's the Power of Partners.

GARVEY
SCHUBERT ▶ the power of partners
BARER

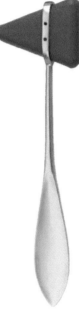

GARVEY HELPS REGENCE BCBS STAY IN GREAT SHAPE.

Garvey Schubert Barer lawyers. We know health care and have partnered with Regence BlueCross BlueShield, serving their legal needs to help keep Oregonians healthy for over 20 years. That's the Power of Partners.

GARVEY SCHUBERT BARER ▶ *the power of partners*

Beijing • New York • Portland • Seattle • Washington, DC • www.gsblaw.com • 503.228.3939

•••

Testimonials are particularly effective for smaller or lesser-known firms that have an impressive client roster, because it leverages the credibility of their better-known clients. In representing Forde Law, a small Chicago litigation firm, we discovered that they had a stable of powerhouse clients. For example, they successfully defended President Obama's former Chief of Staff Rahm Emanuel in the case where he sought to establish Chicago residency in order to run for Mayor. Impressive.

Perhaps even more credible was Forde Law's representation of the Federal Judges Association in a case in which the judges sought a raise in their pay. Judges obviously know the best trial lawyers; they're practicing in their courtrooms every day. And if they choose to hire *your* law firm, that's something you might want to shout from the rooftops. Which, of course, is precisely what we did.

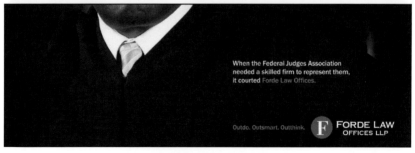

Testimonials work. Ask anyone.

DEMOGRAPHIC

LEVENFELD PEARLSTEIN

Law firms with visionary leaders often take risks to break new ground in the profession, ushering in change—often much-needed change. One extremely effective strategy is to identify an underserved demographic and seek to become the market leader in serving their needs. How do you identify these underserved groups? Certainly, you can conduct research or study demographic changes in the marketplace. And sometimes it's just being smart enough to recognize a good idea when it comes along.

In 2000, two small, old-line, Chicago firms merged to create a new middle-market firm, Levenfeld Pearlstein, led by dynamic, business-oriented chairman, Bryan Schwartz. One evening Bryan watched a made-for-TV movie called "If These Walls Could Talk 2," in which the death of an elderly lesbian woman led to disastrous legal problems for her lifelong partner. Upon her death, the deceased woman's estranged family swooped in and took everything. After all, their relationship had no contractual support.

Levenfeld Pearlstein had one of Chicago's leading tax and estate planning practices, and Bryan recognized that there could have been a legal solution to this woman's plight, if she'd only known and availed herself of the assistance. Bryan excitedly called me at home late that night and said, "We could have *helped* her!" We met the next morning to strategize how to target this audience.

He had identified a gap in the marketplace, that is, serving the unique legal needs of gay and lesbian business owners, the nation's first such practice group.

Schwartz and his partners positioned the gay-rights practice group to zero in on the unique business and legal needs of the gay and lesbian communities—a bold and progressive decision at the time. After all, this was a decade and a half before the Supreme Court issued its landmark ruling stating that the Constitution requires that same-sex couples be allowed to marry no matter where they live and that states may no longer reserve the right only for heterosexual couples.

As absurd as it seems now, this initiative was viewed as extremely risky. After all, not all of the firm's clients were as progressive as Bryan, and no one could predict how the client base would respond. Positively or negatively? Would it generate sizable dollars, or lose the firm major clients? After discussing it internally, the firm decided that it was simply the right thing to do … and damn the torpedoes.

Schwartz asked my team and me to help launch this practice, designing and implementing a positioning and branding campaign targeted to these gay and lesbian families (the LGBTQ abbreviation was not yet in widespread use). The multi-faceted campaign included print ads, a brochure, direct mailers, seminars, conferences, and public relations. We went all out, in part because we knew that this was an important demographic to serve—one with many legal needs—and that we were riding the swelling crest of a socially historic wave.

We were able to use this campaign to garner significant national media attention in the legal, business, and gay press, further solidifying the firm's image as a creative, progressive group of legal service providers. We decided to use the second-person "you" and "your" to appeal directly to these communities that for so many years had confronted daily discrimination. This helped with inclusivity and was important to the message. We went with these ad headlines:

"All couples need to talk about the future. Gay and lesbian couples need to talk to a lawyer about it."

"The law does not recognize your relationship. But there is a law firm that does."

And, here's one of the visuals:

**You can finally talk about the future.
Now plan for it.**

Levenfeld Pearlstein. Not your everyday firm.

Levenfeld Pearlstein, LLC | Chicago • Northfield | www.lplegal.com

CLIENT SERVICE

LANER MUCHIN

Consider this twenty-first century irony. In today's instant-gratification, immediate-communication, texting, emailing, FaceTiming and Skyping, fast-paced, back-and-forth world, one in which a Google search pops up answers to your questions in seconds, law firm clients still wait … and wait … and wait … for their lawyers to return phone calls.

In every single survey of the legal profession since the 1980s, "inadequate responsiveness" has been one of law firm clients' biggest complaints. "I just want my lawyer to call me back!" they wail.

A law firm in Chicago gets it, and they have provided an astonishing level of responsiveness for 40 years. A highly regarded labor and employment boutique, Laner Muchin is likely The World's Most Responsive Law Firm. They always call every client back, every time, in *two hours or less*. This wasn't a formal written policy and they didn't really talk about it; it was simply the personal standard of the firm's founder, Dick Laner. This was how the partners remembered life as an associate at Laner Muchin: "God help you if you didn't return Dick's clients' calls within two hours."

And with negligible attorney turnover, the Laner Muchin lawyers didn't really understand that their two-hour standard was truly remarkable in the legal profession. Most firms back then had a loose, unenforced 24-hour call-return policy, or more commonly, no policy at all. *Try* to return the clients' calls within 24 hours, but if you didn't, it wasn't a big deal—the clients would wait. But they seethed.

I persuaded Laner Muchin that this attribute was actually a very big deal—that clients switched law firms based upon frustration with client service and responsiveness. We could set up Laner Muchin as the legitimate alternative, when their highly skilled labor and employment firm simply failed to provide good service.

In 2003, working in close collaboration with Fishman Marketing, the Laner Muchin partners launched their two-hour phone call commitment—to significant fanfare within the profession. Dozens of feature stories were written about this firm's remarkable level of responsiveness.

The deal was, and still is today, a pledge from all the lawyers in the firm to return phone calls within two hours—and less if you specify that it's an emergency. If a lawyer can't meet the pledge, because, say, she's in a negotiation or on a three-hour flight, she will have followed the firm's protocol and arranged for a colleague to cover for her, and secretaries will regularly check the lawyers' voicemail. The commitment works internally too; lawyers and staff have to return their colleagues' calls within two hours.

Here's how the responsive service guarantee came about. During our interviews with attorneys, we discovered that they took pride in returning client calls quickly—it was an important service attribute—so we used it as the centerpiece of the firm's marketing. Together with the firm's internal training team, we conducted firm-wide responsiveness programs, and the firm purchased costly new technology to ensure they could meet this rigorous service commitment. They were already at 95 percent or more compliance; to go national with this commitment, they wanted to do even better.

Working closely with marketing partner Joe Yastrow, one of the nation's top employment lawyers, we created supporting collateral materials, including a revised firm logo (that included a stylized clock), a firm brochure, a Two-Hour brochure, new website, and an extensive public relations campaign to build buzz.

My favorite part was the "Laner Muchin Challenge," which throws down the gauntlet, *daring* prospects to see how their existing lawyers' responsiveness compares to ours:

> *If you're currently represented by a different employment law firm, you can experience the Laner Muchin difference. Take the Laner Muchin Challenge:*

Call your current lawyer and leave a message to return your call. Wait an hour or two (to give your lawyer a decent head start), then call one of our lawyers and leave the same message. See who calls you back first; we're betting it'll be us. If it's not, we'll buy you lunch and donate $100 to your favorite charity.

The beauty of The Challenge is that there's no downside for the firm. Of course they'll call you back within two hours; it's what they do, so they'll always look good. But if the client's existing law firm nonetheless calls back first, for a $100 charitable donation, the Laner lawyers get to take someone else's client out for lunch. (I was particularly proud of that part.)

We later mailed foot-tall, hand-blown, hour-long hourglasses directly to prospects to encourage them to take The Challenge. We encouraged the recipients to keep our message and the Laner lawyers' contact information on their desks year-round. The mailing achieved a direct-response rate exceeding 50 percent. The campaign received the Legal Marketing Association's grand prize in 2006, the optional Best of Show award.

WE'RE SMART. WE'RE OLD. AND WE'RE THE BEST AT EVERYTHING.

RELIGION

SCHLAPPRIZZI LAW

In some cases, a strong and distinctive culture can help define a firm's marketing and effectively target a particular niche demographic. But what if a firm's culture is distinctly religious?

Religion is often viewed as the third-rail of marketing, something to be avoided at all costs. In recent decades, most law firm Christmas cards have become holiday cards. There are legitimate arguments regarding whether it's appropriate to bring religion into a workplace, and I'm intending to stay quite far away from that discussion.

Schlapprizzi Law is a leading personal injury and medical malpractice firm in the St. Louis area. Not surprisingly, personal injury is a cutthroat, competitive specialty. Mass-marketing firms spend a fortune every year on broadcast advertising and publicity tools such as billboards and online keyword marketing.

The Schlapprizzi lawyers had invited me to their office just before Christmas. When I walked in, I was immediately struck by the beautiful lobby, festively decorated floor to ceiling in bright red and silver. One table featured a large nativity scene. This was the largest Christmas display I'd ever seen at a law firm and, apparently, this was the firm's annual tradition. It unapologetically expressed the firm's religious culture and personality.

As we've previously discussed, when you have a smaller budget, it's helpful to focus. You might find that focus in a target audience, industry, or geography, perhaps, or a specialty practice niche.

Some personal injury firms have learned to focus on bringing in certain types of cases, like birth-related injuries, dog bites, or motorcycle accidents. And, of course, we've all seen the TV ads. *Have you been injured in a such-and-such accident? Do you suffer from horrible condition X brought on by harmful drug Y or faulty medical device Z?*

After conducting extensive interviews with the Schlapprizzi professionals, we decided to aim at an audience that was true to the firm culture. A father and his two children are the firm's principals. The mother, the firm's business manager, hosts a popular half-hour weekly program on local Catholic radio. We realized that the family's sincere dedication to their church and faith made them a particularly good legal option for community members with similar beliefs. The Schlapprizzi family lawyers understand this group and shares their values, views, and traditions. That common ground would help them serve Catholic clients in a familiar and comfortable way.

Recognizing the firm's strong Catholic faith and its connection with that religious community as the marketing hook we should use, we began a campaign that appealed to that slice of the population. The goal: Make Schlapprizzi the go-to firm for the area's seriously injured Catholics. We created a marketing campaign to define Schlapprizzi as "outstanding injury lawyers who are committed to representing those of the Catholic faith."

With a multi-media approach, we produced print ads targeting the local archdiocese weekly newspaper and bi-monthly magazine. We also developed a small, inexpensive microsite, CatholicInjuryLaw. com, illustrated with the same visuals. Additionally, we ran banner ads and 30-second radio spots read by Mrs. Schlapprizzi, the firm's very own radio personality.

To support the primary print campaign and add interest and name recognition, we also designed some low-priced but effective strip ads that leveraged the firm's unique name, including a phonetically spelled version.

PROFESSIONAL ASSOCIATION
LITIGATION COUNSEL OF AMERICA (LCA)

Professional associations vary in quality. Most are good, but some are great, serving their members brilliantly and providing great opportunities to broaden the horizon of the profession for which it exists.

The Litigation Counsel of America (LCA) is in the "great" category—in fact, I think it's one of the most remarkable associations in the legal profession. The 3,500-member LCA is a combined honorary, social/networking, educational, and referral organization for trial lawyers primarily in the insurance industry. It more accurately could be called "The Nation's Best Trial Lawyers Association."

The group's membership (the "Fellows") comprises outstanding attorneys—peer-selected, vigorously vetted trial lawyers, both plaintiff and defense. If you need a rock-solid attorney for your dispute, you can't go wrong with hiring one of the LCA attorneys—they're prequalified.

When the LCA came to us for help with their marketing efforts, our objective was clear: Build visibility and brand recognition to generate referrals for these leading trial lawyers from thousands of different law firms.

We wanted to communicate to the purchasers of legal service that LCA attorneys are carefully scrutinized, broadly experienced legal leaders in their field. We also wanted to let potential clients know that LCA Fellows weren't all fellows, nor were they all white. The association was established with the mission of supporting and advancing women and minorities, whom the founder, Steve Henry, believed were being unfairly excluded from other honorary litigation associations.

My team and I wanted to make sure the LCA distinguished itself from similar or lesser organizations in the profession. We needed a clear, clever, and concise way to describe this in a tag line, brand message, and visual imagery. The challenge was that the full name was too long, and we've already discussed at length why we generally hate initials. Most of LCA's top competitors also have long names and are known by litigators by their initials, for example FDCC, PLAC, and IADC.

Further, the logo LCA had been using was too big and complex, starting with (1) an artistic but illegible treatment of the initials that many referred to as "the beer mug," then (2) a simpler rendition of "LCA," (3) a tag line, "In Honor of Excellence," (4) the entire organization name, "Litigation Counsel of America," and finally (5) a descriptor, "Trial Lawyer Honorary Society." It was just too, too much.

Without a reasonable alternative, we compromised by creating a logo that included a short tag line, "Proven Trial Lawyers," that informed viewers what "LCA" is, allowing us to drastically increase the name's point size. Where possible, we also try to include the organization's full name somewhere nearby.

The brand message suggests the significant trial skills that LCA Fellows possess: "A trial lawyer is just a trial lawyer. Unless she's an LCA Fellow." The website is dramatically illustrated by black-and-white, heavily shadowed noir photos of the actual Fellows, which we shot over time at LCA conferences.

The branding package went over quite well with LCA members and the legal-service-buying public.

What do you think?

before

after

LEGAL ASSOCIATION

INTERNATIONAL LAWYERS NETWORK

Clearly we live in a global world—everyone's going global. In fact, I bet you can't get through a single meeting without hearing that word: *Global* economy. *Global* network. *Global* platform. *Global* marketplace. And certainly, most mid-sized and large law firms must have *global* reach. If not, they risk being considered provincial and won't get much work from companies that might need legal service outside of the United States.

That's why, of course, many firms have offices in London, Paris, Dubai, Shanghai, Tokyo, Buenos Aires… you get the idea. But not all can or should open a shop overseas, even though their clients need help in foreign markets. That's where global legal associations come to the rescue. These associations of independent law firms exist to network, share referrals across local or international jurisdictions, and form helpful inter-firm social relationships.

There are hundreds of such organizations configured in many different ways. Some focus on particular practice areas, like litigation or labor and employment law. Others require that the member firms must be single-office general practice firms, or among the largest firms in their particular market. Some are close-knit and professionally managed, while others are less structured. Among the largest and finest of the general practice networks is the International Lawyers Network.

ILN has 5,000 member lawyers practicing in 90 law firms in 70 countries. Like all networks, they need to regularly remind the member firms' less-active lawyers of their membership, to generate additional intra-network referrals. But we know that lawyers are busy and uninterested; they're unlikely to take the time to read a newsletter or other traditional methods of conveying this type of information. Heck, they don't even read their own law firms' materials.

Too often lawyers deride their firms' valuable membership in an in-

WE'RE SMART. WE'RE OLD. AND WE'RE THE BEST AT EVERYTHING.

ternational network as "That's just Joe's international boondoggle." We needed to remind the lawyers more regularly and memorably of the firm's membership, so it came to mind when an opportunity arose to send a referral to a firm in another local or international jurisdiction.

Lindsay Griffiths, ILN's Director of Global Relationship Management, came to us for help in spreading the word about, well, spreading the word. She wanted a creative campaign to reach deeper into ILN's member firms without requiring the lawyers to invest much time. We needed to design a marketing strategy that would grab their attention and convey the information quickly and cost effectively.

So, naturally, we went with stickers.

Let me explain. We created a series of light-tack stickers that could be applied to the firms' bathroom mirrors. On them were images of hats stereotypically representing different countries, like cowboy hats for the United States or conical straw hats (also called rice hats) worn in some Asian countries. Anyone standing at the sink would appear as though they were wearing the hat—the idea of course was to reinforce the international message.

A second sticker, placed below the various hats, depicted text, in the imperative mood, which directed the person standing before the mirror to: *"Imagine you need a lawyer in China."* (Or whatever country correlated with the hat.)

Imagine you need a lawyer in China.
Your International Lawyers Network.

www.ILN.com

In a second series, we had life-sized stickers of people from all over the world who, when affixed to the mirrors, would seem to be standing at the next sink. The headline: *"International Lawyers Network. We're always with you."*

Finally, we had seven-foot stickers of doorways that seemed to open to various parts of the world, which could be stuck temporarily to the law firms' walls. The text read: *"You belong to the International Lawyers Network. Welcome to the world."*

In all of these, the powerful and unavoidable visuals conveyed the messages in just a glance; they did not require the lawyers to invest their time in reading some marketing literature. And they were immediately unforgettable—the lawyers needn't see them a second time to remember them. They only needed to be stuck to the mirrors or lobby wall for a day or two to be effective. And when another version was used the next week or month, it magnified the total impact.

We felt the strategy was extremely powerful—and we weren't the only ones. The campaign won a Legal Marketing Association "Best of Show" award. One judge said, "We should all agree to move this one to Best of Show before continuing the rest of the judging."

It was a unanimous vote.

RECRUITING LAW STUDENTS

FENWICK & WEST

At the height of the Dot Com Boom, Silicon Valley-based Fenwick & West had a problem most law firms would die for: Their workload was overflowing; they had too much business.

I know, that doesn't sound like anything the firm leaders would lose sleep over today. But when this dynamic partnership, which had positioned itself as one of the nation's most skilled high-tech firms, needed to boost its 250-lawyer ranks, they encountered fierce competition for talent. Good young lawyers were in high demand. And, with an over-abundance of the most cutting-edge Silicon Valley matters, they were being forced to decline challenging work from sophisticated clients.

The firm desperately needed to recruit and hire dozens of top law school graduates and get them into the Fenwick pipeline. Making the situation more desperate was the three-month window. On-campus recruiting would be starting very soon.

The firm's outstanding CMO, Diane Hamlin, came to us to help the firm overcome a curious challenge: Despite offering some of the nation's most intriguing, high-tech-related work in a culture legitimately renowned for its collegiality, Fenwick was having difficulty with its law school recruiting efforts. They were looking to hire the top students at the top law schools, but couldn't fill the slots in their on-campus interviews.

So I traveled around the country, interviewing students many of the top-ranked law schools, to discover why so many of them were avoiding Fenwick. It turns out the students misperceived what a "high-tech firm" was. They thought Fenwick was like a patent firm, which required a college degree in engineering or other hard science to qualify, so they ignored Fenwick when they came to campus. (In reality, most Fenwick lawyers held liberal arts degrees.)

To dispel that myth, we worked closely with Diane and the firm's exceptional marketing and recruiting groups and outside advertising agency. In a true collaborative effort, we created a comprehensive marketing campaign to attract the best-and-brightest students to the firm. We deployed a barrage of marketing tools—advertising, a revised website, public relations, online marketing, giveaways, on-campus activities, and many others. You name it, we did it.

We used headlines like these to draw people in and persuade them that we were looking for law students B.A.'s, not just B.S. degrees:

"High-tech law at Fenwick & West. It's not just for geeks."

"If you have great grades and your VCR isn't flashing 12:00..."

That text and the rest of our outreach generated great results. In the first three-month recruiting season, the firm's summer-associate class more than *doubled*, from 29 to 71 top students, while maintaining extremely rigorous academic and interpersonal standards.

And here is one of the ads we produced:

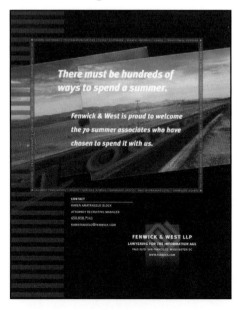

DIVERSITY

CARLTON FIELDS
CONSTANGY, BROOKS

Most law firms recognize the need to increase and maximize their diversity, for several reasons. Lawyers from a variety of backgrounds bring unique outlooks and broader networks of connections. Multilingual capabilities strengthen a firm's appeal. A non-homogenous firm tends to encourage creativity and innovative solutions. And then there are the corporate clients: They expect the firms they retain to look like them, that is, diverse. All of these factors help improve the bottom line.

When it comes to law firms, though, "increasing diversity" is much easier said than done. They often struggle to recruit and retain women and minority attorneys and professionals. And assimilating new perspectives into an existing culture can be a challenge.

With law firms slow to change, clients have been driving much of the focus on diversity. Large companies began using their legal budgets as leverage, demanding that their law firms quickly increase their numbers of women and minority lawyers. In a panic, many firms began boldly embracing diversity—or at least the abstract concept of it—emphasizing the sincerity of their efforts with $20 stock photos of conference rooms filled with awkwardly posed men and women of different ethnic backgrounds.

If your firm has a credible story to tell, and many do, now is a good time to tell it. One such firm is Florida-based Carlton, Fields, Emmanuel, Smith & Cutler (which is now called Carlton Fields Jorden Burt after a regional merger)

By way of background, a decade ago Carlton Fields hired Fishman Marketing to support the firm's diversity initiative. We were asked to interview name partner Reece Smith and elicit and share some of the firm's historic landmark cases.

WE'RE SMART. WE'RE OLD. AND WE'RE THE BEST AT EVERYTHING.

I learned that these included fighting against lynchings in 1920, "inventing" telecommuting for a pregnant partner on bed rest in the 1960s, integrating an all-white private club in 1973, hiring Jewish and Native American lawyers back when Protestant firms wouldn't, and more. It was a stunning list of precedents. These stories needed to be told.

But first, they needed to be noticed. So we designed a collection of brightly colored ads with powerful, almost shocking headlines. When you have the facts, use the facts. Proving your commitment with actual evidence is more persuasive than high-flying platitudes. Here are a few examples.

Atlanta's Constangy, Brooks, Smith & Prophete is one of the nation's largest labor and employment law firms, with lawyers across 29 offices. As I mentioned in Chapter 8, when I was discussing logos, we represented the firm in its intentional, strategic, top-down initiative to increase its diversity.

The firm's campaign was a resounding success, and deserves a few more words here.

Constangy's leadership saw an opportunity to take the lead in diversity among its top L&E competitors. They simultaneously hired dozens of skilled lawyers nationwide who were diverse in background, thought, gender, and ethnicity.

We helped the firm develop its marketing strategy, create a new brand and logo (recall the camera lens with the "A wider lens on workplace law" tag line), and produced fresh marketing and advertising materials to reflect the firm's inclusive push.

We launched ads showing a striking composite image of smiling, confident lawyers and professionals, with the headline, "This is what labor & employment law looks like in the 21st century."

WE'RE SMART. WE'RE OLD. AND WE'RE THE BEST AT EVERYTHING.

The materials won first place for Best Identity Campaign in the Legal Marketing Association's 2015 Southeast Chapter Your Honor Awards, and second place at the LMA's national awards.

Better yet, Constangy has been able to attract more lawyers that help the firm expand its diversity even more broadly. Firms that authentically show their commitment make recruiting like-minded people even easier. Consequently, the firm continues to pull in top-of-the-line sophisticated clients—who like what they see.

HISTORY

COOPER ERVING & SAVAGE

Some firms like to market their "proud history and tradition." Normally, I'm not a big fan of this strategy. My argument to firms that have used this comes down to the fact that no law firm prospect has ever said,

"You know what I'm looking for in my law firm? Longevity. If I could just find an old firm, that's the firm I'd hire."

At this point, the law firms tend to counter with a "stability" argument, that having been around for 25, 50, or 100 years suggests that they'll be around for another 25, 50, or 100—that they must be doing something right. And during a tumultuous time of rapid law firm mergers, acquisitions, and implosions, there's something to be said for a sense of permanency.

That's not a bad argument, but at the rate that historic old firms have been merging and collapsing lately, I don't know of any data that support that argument. Further, in the past few decades I've interviewed hundreds of clients, sat through countless client panel discussions, and read a lot of market research, and I can't recall any clients identifying "proud tradition" or "endurance" as a statistically significant hiring issue.

Now I'm not against celebrating round-number anniversaries, like 10, 20, 25, 50, 75, and 100. In fact, I advocate it. I think we have too few reasons to celebrate inside law firms. We should grab every opportunity to have fun together, even if we're just making them up. I think we should party more and find ways to bond with all personnel—it helps create a nicer culture.

So, normally I'd advise you to celebrate your firm's history to enhance morale, not client development. That is, unless there's something truly unique or special about your history. An example of a firm with a

WE'RE SMART. WE'RE OLD. AND WE'RE THE BEST AT EVERYTHING.

very special history is Albany's Cooper Erving & Savage. They're 232 years old, the second-oldest law firm in the United States, boasting a remarkable pedigree.

The firm's story was the story of upstate New York, with their founders and families tied countless ways to the region's early growth. The "Cooper" in Cooper Erving was Paul Cooper, the son of James Fenimore Cooper, the famed author of *The Last of the Mohicans* (1826), one of America's great historical novels.

When I first met Cooper Erving, the firm was 201 years old, and called seeking a branding upgrade. They had recently signed another three-year website contract with FindLaw that they couldn't break, so they hired us to rebrand their cliché-filled site. Cooper Erving was a remarkable firm with a thoroughly unremarkable website, illustrated by people, a building, and columns. <yawn>

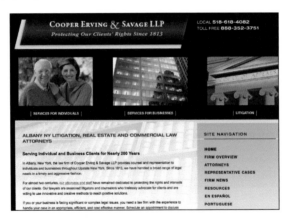

In a case of marketing malpractice, they'd neglected to celebrate their 200th anniversary. My jaw dropped. But I soon realized that the friendly, skilled, and well-intentioned small firm didn't have any marketing support. In professional-services firms, client demands come first. One thing leads to another, time passes, and non-billable activities slip through the cracks. It's quite common inside small firms.

I told them I'd help. Two hundred years—this was too big an event to miss! So I set them on the task of learning more about their history to help with the press releases and speeches. New online databases had become available, and in the course of conducting this research, they discovered evidence that proved that they were actually 232 years old, founded in 1785, not 1815, which additional research showed made them the nation's second-oldest law firm. That's a pretty big deal. That's worth celebrating.

When visiting the firm, I saw hanging on their conference room wall a fascinating ancient real estate deed with a red wax seal they'd pulled from their firm archives. It was for the transfer of property involving a local Native American tribe. At the bottom, the chief had signed the document using a hand-drawn pictogram of a turtle.

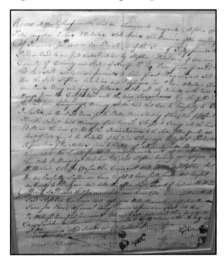

I thought it was important to find a way to help tell the firm's proud story, to connect it to its extraordinary past. We redesigned the firm's logo, adding the scanned pictograph turtle for interest, creating a hook for clients and prospects to inquire about the firm's history. We also knew that we were likely to be able to generate stories in the media about this unique logo, which would increase the buzz about this firm for its history and creativity.

I was confident that we could also persuade some publications to feature the firm's history. The media is always looking for legitimately interesting stories to write about. This was objectively interesting. We only needed to select the right media and bring it to their attention … which we did.

The website is illustrated by "Abduction of Boone's Daughter by the Indians," a famous painting by German-American painter Karl Ferdinand Wimar. It depicts the 1776 capture near Boonesborough, KY of Jemima Boone and two other girls by a Cherokee-Shawnee raiding party. The incident is said to have inspired the chase scene in *The Last of the Mohicans*. The home page headline connects to their history, "We go back to when there was a lot more than one Mohican." The connection to the classic book adds credibility to the firm, like a testimonial—it implies quality.

Whenever incorporating another culture or demographic, it is important to ensure that you are not being insensitive. To avoid an embarrassing accusation of cultural appropriation, the firm ran the revised logo and brand materials by some local Native American friends for their approval.

This type of historical marketing does not express how the Cooper Erving lawyers are superior to others, but it puts the firm solidly on the map. It's the hook that can create a buzz in the community and increase the perception of quality, enhancing the individual marketing of every single lawyer.

After being introduced at a party or conference, rather than "Cooper Erving? Hmm, I've never heard of you guys," the comments become "Cooper Erving? Hey, I know you! Great firm." At that point, the lawyers don't feel like they must defensively validate the quality of their firm with hollow credentialing. And the turtle on the logo is an icebreaker with nearly every recipient.

CONCLUSION: PART TWO

So there you have it, a few dozen law firm case studies reflecting the challenges confronting the powerful but conservative legal sector. Today's economy is robust and roiling; the legal profession is expected to look very different in five or ten years. No one knows precisely how these fluctuations will affect any particular firm, practice, or geography, but history shows that nimble firms tend to weather the upheaval better than complacent firms in the middle.

Some firms will seek to lead, to grow, to prosper.

Will it be you?

ACKNOWLEDGEMENTS

To my loyal clients and lawyer friends. To the attorneys who have opened to me their fears and firms and futures—Managing Partners handling the 30,000-foot view, and Marketing Partners grinding it out day-to-day in the trenches.

And equally to the hard-working **in-house marketing professionals** who strive to do their best, pushing that boulder up the hill every single day, and helping their lawyers and firms succeed. I have had the great honor to work with you for over 25 years.

To my wonderful old friends in NALFMA, and countless newer friends in the **Legal Marketing Association**. We started this preposterous journey together a lifetime ago, creating an entire industry from scratch. Although the faces continue to change, your selfless dedication remains constant. I doubt that a kinder, smarter, or more generous group of professionals exists; I'm so blessed to be part of this community. Similarly, to the **Association of Legal Administrators** and the **College of Law Practice Management,** where I go to mingle with gurus and learn what's new, what's hot, and what's next.

To my friends, peers, clients, and competitors, who always had the time to answer questions and help me learn and improve. To Aleisha, Allan, Amy, Ann, Barbara, Barry, Betsi, Bev, Bill, Bryan, Burkey, Caroline, Carolyn, Cherie, Chris, Darryl, Dave, David, Dean, Deborah, Diane, Donna, Doug, Eileen, Ellen, Eric, Ernie, Felice, Fred, Fred, Gene, Gina, Guido, Halley, Heather, Iris, Jeffrey, Jim, Joe, John, Jon, Jordan, Joy, Julia, Kelly, Kevin, Kim, Kwadwo, Lance, Leigh, Lindsay, Lisa, Lorne, Lynn, Maggie, Marcy, Mark, Martha, Melissa, Merrilyn, Mike, Monte, Nancy, Nat, Nathalie, Nora, Norm, Patty, Ric, Rick, Roberta, Rodger, Russell, Stacey, Stacy, Steph, Steve, Sue-Ella, Suzanne, Sydney, Tanna, Terri, Tim, Tom, Wendy, Will, and so many, many others across the country and around the world.

WE'RE SMART. WE'RE OLD. AND WE'RE THE BEST AT EVERYTHING.

To Gwen, Dennis, Kevin, and Rich, the dynamic marketing committee at Coffield Ungaretti & Harris, who hired me away from Winston & Strawn by saying, "Let's go do something great." And to Beth and Jennifer who helped make it happen.

To my **mother** for her unflinching support (and valuable help proofreading), and my **father** who taught me to never accept "because that's how we've always done it."

To my terrific editors, Steve Taylor and Cindy Collins-Taylor, without whom this material would have forever remained a "solid first draft" but never an actual book.

To Loren Wittner, my first boss and mentor, the legal profession's first Marketing Partner, whose name I serendipitously stumbled over in the morning paper. I called Loren out of the blue, to learn what this "law firm marketing thing" was, and he graciously took my call, invited me in to chat, and *hired* me two weeks later, changing my life forever.

And to John R. Bates who, back in 1977, fought all the way to the US Supreme Court for a lawyer's right to provide truthful, useful marketing information to clients, risking his law license in a principled stand, and making all of this possible.

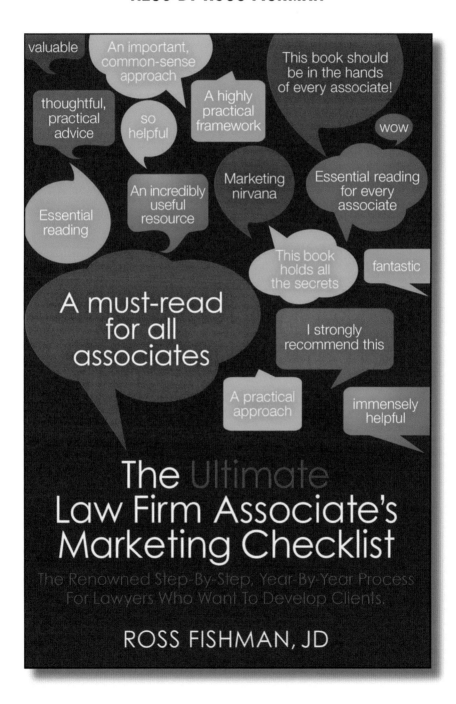

Lawyers—do you want to learn the most efficient way to become a rainmaker?

Marketers—do you need a simple, step-by-step process to help your associates succeed?

Satisfied professionals have called this book "The best marketing tool ever" and "Marketing nirvana!" Dozens of major law firms have ordered hundreds of copies to give to their grateful associates.

Do You Want a Rewarding, Fulfilling Career?
This is the resource you've been waiting for. It's been used for 25 years by law firm associates in their successful quests to become rainmakers.

Marketers, administrators, and professional-development experts call this dramatically expanded 50-page edition "a powerful tool to help associates achieve their potential." It includes new online tools, plus dozens of examples, case studies, and videos. It is the simplest, most-effective tool to ensure your legal team achieves dramatic professional success.

The renowned *Of Counsel* magazine called this book "a well-written, engaging, and very practical guide … a marketing bible" and "the ideal gift to give to your associates."

ORDER YOURS TODAY!
It's available on Amazon at *goo.gl/HsrmbE*. Bulk discounts for 10+ and 50+ copies are available by contacting the author directly at ross@fishmanmarketing.com.

Read the first chapter now:

"The Ultimate Law Firm Associate's Marketing Checklist"

FIRST-YEAR ASSOCIATES

MINDSET:
Become an excellent lawyer.

Your first priority is to learn to be a great lawyer; external marketing isn't important yet. Your only real proactive activity should be ensuring that you don't lose touch with the people you already know. Maintain relationships with friends from college and law school and any organizations you belong to. Create a reminder to make sure that you've had some contact with your chums once per quarter. Your future self will thank you.

This is the year you should create the basic platform you'll be working from over the next few years, the infrastructure you'll gradually expand over time:

☐ Join one local, state, or national **bar association** and get involved in one targeted educational committee within your practice area.
  o   Meet your peers.
  o   Learn your craft.
  o   Invest in your profession.
  o   Your long-term goal should be to chair a small committee during your fifth year of practice.

☐ Read your firm's website, internal website portal, newsletters, LinkedIn or Facebook pages, and other marketing materials to learn about its range of services and clients.
  o   Read your senior associates' and partners' biographies and profiles as well, to learn about their practices and outside interests. This will come in handy later.

☐ Build your personal brand within your law firm. Focus on internal marketing by developing relationships with your firm's lawyers, both inside and outside of your practice area.

☐ Do not spend your career eating lunch at your desk.
Go out at least:

- o *Once each week* with a firm lawyer inside your practice area
- o *Twice each month* with a firm lawyer outside of your practice area
- o *Regularly* with friends and contacts

☐ Always, always, *always* have **business cards** with you; you never know when you're going to meet someone who could later turn into a client or referral source.

- o The box of 250 cards gathering dust in your desk drawer can't help you unless they're with you when you need them.
- o Leave 75–100 in the box at work, then divide up the rest among all of your pants pockets, suit coats, blazers, jackets, overcoats, gym bags, purses, briefcase, backpack, suitcase, roller bag, and glove box.
- o In particular, put a thick stack in your suitcase, so you don't forget them when attending an out-of-state conference.
- o Watch my brief video about business cards at *https://youtu.be/rAA3291QWnQ.*
- o Consider supplementing printed cards with a personal mobile or digital business card that downloads your contact information directly into a recipient's database with a QR code (see mine below).

I use Vizibility (https://vizibility.com/), but there are many other options.

My Vizibility.com QR Code

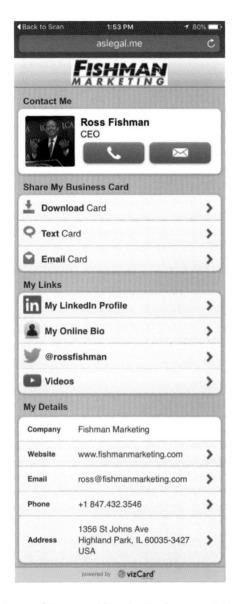

*Scanning my QR code with a simple, free smartphone app,
provides this comprehensive contact information, with live links.*

To avoid embarrassing mix-ups, keep your own cards in your left-side pants or jacket pockets, and the cards you collect on your right side.

☐ Monitor your office visitor list.
  o Stop by and introduce yourself to the firm lawyers visiting from other offices.
  o If there is time and it's appropriate, ask to grab a coffee.

☐ Draft a detailed **website biography**, following the firm's format.
  o Update it regularly, especially when your practice is developing.
  o Ideally you should update it every time a matter you are involved with concludes, you publish an article or give a presentation, are appointed to a committee, etc.
  o Update it thoroughly *at least* every six months.
  o Be judicious in what you include. Delete all items from high school.
  o Be sensible regarding college activities.
  o Delete any *Who's Who* directory "honors" or other questionable accolades. See my blog post at *http://goo.gl/jWrQIY.*

☐ Build your network. **Create a mailing list** of friends and contacts. Opt for more, rather than fewer people, when deciding whom to add.
  o Law school classmates
  o Childhood, high school, and college friends
  o Former colleagues
  o Community association and professional club contacts
  o Parents of your children's friends and contacts through your children's activities

☐ Keep in touch with your existing network, leveraging both traditional and online tools.
- o Events, newsletters, holiday cards, breakfasts, lunches, drinks, phone calls
- o Social media, e.g., LinkedIn, Facebook, Twitter, etc., below.

facebook.

☐ If you don't have a **Facebook** page already, create one.
- o If you *do* have a Facebook page from college, law school, etc., do a thorough audit to ensure it is now professional.
- o Update your security settings.
- o Hide the party photos, etc.
- o Sanitize it so there's nothing a 65-year-old client or the most conservative senior partner would find offensive.
- o Keep it casual and sensible.
- o Check it at least weekly, from home.
- o Join your law school alumni Facebook group.
- o Connect with your friends, especially those from law school.

☐ If you don't have a **LinkedIn** page already, create one.
- o If you do have a LinkedIn page from college or law school, do a thorough audit to ensure it is now professional.
- o Sanitize it so there's nothing a 65-year-old client or the most conservative senior partner would find offensive.
- o Fill it out completely, including the Summary, Contact Information, Experience, and Education sections. Infuse it with your personality.
- o Add a professional photo.
- o Write in the first person and use a friendly, professional tone.

o   Create a custom public profile URL.
o   No one expects it to be very long; you've only been a lawyer for a few minutes.
o   Review the privacy settings.
o   Check it weekly.
o   Post occasional relevant Updates, including thought leadership pieces you have written.
o   It's easy to start by sharing or liking things that others in your firm have posted.
o   Remember, listening and engaging with what others post is as important in social networking as what you say and post.
o   Join your law school LinkedIn alumni group and your firm's LinkedIn group.
o   Consider starting a group for your graduation class.
o   Build your LinkedIn network; connect with friends, peers, co-workers, acquaintances, and classmates.
o   Regularly "Endorse" clients, friends, peers, co-workers, and prospects; it only takes a click. They'll typically endorse you back.
o   A word of caution with Skills and Endorsements: When you receive an endorsement from someone for a specific skill, only post it on your bio if you have actual expertise in that area. Some state bar rules have restrictions on this.
    • When in doubt, leave it off.

☐ If you don't have a **Twitter** account, create one under your name.
o   Check it occasionally, from home.
o   Build your Twitter network; connect with contacts and thought leaders.
o   Post at least weekly on something relating to your job or interests.

- o Re-tweet tweets that resonate with you.
- o Consider utilizing Twitter as a listening platform to better understand clients, prospects, competitors, scholars, and more.
- o Pay attention to what they are promoting, discussing, commenting on. It can all be valuable.
- o Follow people, companies, associations, and organizations within your legal, business, and general areas of interest.

☐ Sign up for **Google Alerts** at google.com/alerts. See video at *https://goo.gl/bAeQhj*.
- o For the Search Terms, use "[your name]" and "[your firm's name]" (in quotes).
- o Consider also creating alerts on friends, relatives, and prospects.
- o Drop them a quick email when you see them mentioned.
- o Even more powerful is a short handwritten note (more on this to follow).

☐ Create a comprehensive personal **Google+** profile.
- o Go to *https://profiles.google.com/me*
  - • Mine's at *https://plus.google.com/+RossFishman*
- o Google highly ranks Google+ profiles in name searches.
- o Add links to your Facebook, LinkedIn, and Twitter accounts.

☐ Before you engage in any marketing or social media, review
- o Your firm's social media policy
- o Your state's ethics rules governing the use of marketing, communication, and social media (generally Rules 7.1–7.4; see *http://goo.gl/JOhhF*)

☐ Develop a reputation for providing the highest-quality

client service.

o Remember, the profession is full of smart, technically skilled lawyers.

  - The lawyers clients value are those who excel at communication, timeliness, and accessibility.

o Keep clients regularly informed regarding the current status of their matters.

  - Send them copies of all relevant correspondence.

o *Always* call clients back promptly, ideally within two hours.

  - Consider: if you have a sick child, how would you feel about a pediatrician who has an "All calls returned within 24 hours" policy?

  - If you are unavailable (e.g. on a plane, in court, etc.), train your secretary to check your phone messages regularly.

    o Have him/her return the client's call.

    o Explain that you will be unavailable until a particular time. Ask if they would like their call returned then, or if they would prefer having someone else address the issue sooner.

o Give clients and prospects your cell phone number.

  - They will appreciate the offer and won't abuse the privilege with late night or weekend calls.

o Check your email at least once every night and on weekends.

FISHMAN
MARKETING

Ross Fishman, J.D.
CEO

Blogs:
FishmanMarketing.com/blog
LawFirmSpeakers.com

Twitter: @rossfishman
LinkedIn.com/in/rossfishman

1356 St. Johns Avenue
Highland Park, IL 60035 USA
+1.847.432.3546 [847.HEADLINE]
Ross@FishmanMarketing.com

FishmanMarketing.com